GLUTEN FREE AROUND the WORLD

aviva kanoff

a journey of food, travel & extraordinary adventure

breakfast

- Blueberry Scones 11
- Coconut Pancakes 13
- Crêpes ... Lemon Curd & Fresh Berries .. 15
- Irish Soda Corn Bread 17
- Lemon Ricotta Pancakes 19
- Onion Lover's Spinach Scramble 20
- Shakshuka 23

pg. 41

soups & salads

- 4 Bean & Kale Super Stew 27
- Beef Pho 28
- Black Bean & Corn Salad 31
- Candied Fig & Goat Cheese Salad 33
- Chestnut Soup 34
- Curried Quinoa Salad with Mint Raita ... 37
- Curried Yam Soup 39
- Feta Cheese & Quinoa Salad 41
- Irish Blue Potato Beef Stew 43
- Italian Wedding Soup 45
- Mandarin Orange Chicken Salad 46
- Moroccan Mint Beet Salad 49
- Pepper Steak Salad 51
- Pomegranate & Goat Cheese Salad 53
- Sweet Potato Leek Soup 54
- Thai Beef Salad 57

pg. 111

sides

- Baby Bok Choy with Garlic & Ginger 61
- Bhinidi Masala 63
- Bocaditos de Papa 65
- Ginger Brown Rice 67
- Indian Spiced Roasted Chickpeas 68
- Irish Garlic Brussels Sprouts 71
- Layered Ratatouille 72
- Lemon Jerra Rice 74
- Maple Ginger Roasted Sweet Potatoes ... 76
- Mexican Street Corn 79
- Nutty Corn Pancakes 80
- Plantain Chips 82
- Saffron Rice 85
- Sesame Garlic String Beans 87
- Spanish Quinoa with Sausages 88
- Spicy Diakon Radish Fries 91
- Spinach & Quinoa Fritters 93
- Veggie Pakoras 95

vegetarian

- Aloo Gobi 99
- Bhurtha 101
- Butternut Squash Gnocchi 102
- Chana Masala 105
- Coconut Da'al 107
- Eggplant Parmigiana 108
- Eggplant Risotto 111
- Garlic & Basil Spaghetti Squash 112
- Malai Kofta 115
- Palak Paneer 117
- Pasta with Spinach & Arugula Pesto 118
- Quinoa Veggie Biryani 120
- Rainbow Quesadilla Pizza 123
- Sage & Onion Spaghetti Squash Soufflé .. 125
- Tofu in Black Bean Sauce 126
- Vegetable Dhansak 129
- Vegetable Jalfrezi 130

fish

- Fish Tacos with Creamed Corn 134
- Halibut al Spinachi 137
- Moroccan Baked Salmon ... Herb Relish 138
- Olive Tapenade Roasted Salmon 141
- Pineapple Salmon Skewers 143
- Plantain Crusted Red Snapper 145
- Rosemary Walnut Salmon ... Garlic Aioli 147
- Tuscan Tuna Steaks ... Basil Yogurt Sauce 148

poultry

- Baked Chicken with Apple & Fennel 153
- Chicken Breasts with Fig-Mustard Glaze .. 155
- Chicken Tikka Masala 156
- Chicken with Mango Ginger Chutney 158
- Coconut Crusted Chicken ... Plum Sauce ... 161
- Coq au Vin with Saffron Quinoa 163
- Duck à l'Orange 164
- Garlic & Almond Chicken 167
- Grilled Chicken with Spicy Mango Salsa ... 169
- Lemongrass Chicken Skewers 171
- Mediterranean Chicken 173
- Moroccan Chicken 174
- Nasi Goreng 176
- Pad Thai 179
- Pineapple Mint Chicken 180
- Tandoori Chicken 182

meat

- Beef Korma 187
- Beef Tacos 189
- Fajitas al Sombrero 191
- Filet Mignon ... Fresh Herb & Garlic Rub .. 192
- Keema 194
- Lamb Curry 197
- Pistachio Mint Crusted Rack of Lamb 199
- Plum & Ginger Brisket 200
- Rosemary Lamb Skewers 203
- Southwestern Meatballs 205
- Truffled Mushroom Silver Tip Roast 207

pg. 203

desserts

- Bailey's Irish Mousse 211
- Banana Walnut Cake 212
- Blueberry Crumble 215
- Chocolate Mousse Pie 217
- Churros 218
- Classic Crème Brûlée 221
- Coconut Cream Parfait 222
- Coconut Sticky Rice with Mango 224
- Irish Apple Cake 227
- Lemon Meringue Tart 228
- Tiramisu 231

I can't believe it's gluten free!

Shown below are just a few of my favorite gluten free products. These products are usually available at your local grocery store and can be found on-line. While you can use whatever products you like, these ones have helped me create some delicious meals!

King Arthur Flour
Gluten Free
Multi-Purpose Flour
24 oz. (680g)

Jeff Nathan Creations
Gluten Free
Panko Flakes
(Seasoned or Plain)
14 oz. (397g)

Tofutti
Gluten & Milk Free
Sour Cream
12 oz. (340g)

Tamari
Gluten Free
Premium Soy Sauce
10 oz. (296mL)

Lundberg
Gluten Free
Rotini Brown Rice Pasta
10 oz. (284g)

Bob's Red Mill
Gluten Free
All Purpose Baking Flour
44 oz. (1.24kg)

Breakfast

London, England

blueberry scones

yield: 10-11 scones

ingredients

- 2 large eggs
- ⅓ cup milk or coconut milk
- 2 tbsp. lemon juice
- 1 tsp. pure vanilla extract
- 1 ¾ cups gluten free all-purpose flour
- ¼ cup granulated sugar
- 2 tsp. baking powder
- ½ tsp. xanthan gum
- ½ tsp. salt
- ¼ tsp. nutmeg (optional)
- ½ cup unsalted cold butter, cut into chunks
- 1 cup fresh blueberries

Topping:
- 2 tsp. granulated sugar (optional)
- 1 tsp. cinnamon (optional)
- butter and blueberry jam (optional)

directions

1. Preheat oven to 400°. Grease a divided scone pan or large muffin pan.
2. Whisk together eggs, milk or coconut milk, lemon juice, and vanilla until frothy.
3. In a separate bowl, sift together flour, sugar, baking powder, xanthan gum, salt, and nutmeg, if using.
4. Using your hands, work in cold butter until the mixture is crumbly.
5. Combine the wet and dry ingredients, stirring until well blended. Then using a spatula, carefully fold in blueberries. The dough should be cohesive and very sticky.
6. Drop dough by the ¼ cupful into the scone or muffin pan. Sprinkle scones with sugar or cinnamon sugar if desired. Let scones rest for 15 minutes.
7. Bake until golden brown, about 15-20 minutes. Remove from oven and let rest for 5 minutes before serving. Best enjoyed warm with butter and blueberry jam.

Bangkok, Thailand

coconut pancakes

yield: 2 servings (6 pancakes)

ingredients

- 1 ¾ cups rice flour
- a pinch of salt
- 1 tbsp. baking powder
- 2 large eggs
- 2 cups coconut milk
- 3-4 tbsp. granulated sugar or agave nectar
- coconut oil for frying
- ¼ cup packaged sweetened shredded coconut

directions

1. In a small bowl, combine flour, salt, and baking powder.
2. In a separate bowl, combine eggs, coconut milk, and sugar or agave nectar. Whisk to dissolve sugar and break up yolks. Pour the wet mixture into the dry mixture and whisk until the batter is smooth.
3. Heat a small frying pan over medium-high heat without oil for at least 1 minute or until pan is hot. This will help to keep the pancakes from sticking to the pan.
4. Add a little oil (about ½ tsp.) and swirl it around the pan. Use a spatula to ensure oil covers all surfaces.
5. Add about ¼ cup batter (use more or less depending on how large or thick you want your pancakes), tilting the pan this way and that to distribute the batter and create a round pancake.
6. Allow the batter to cook at least 1 minute or until small holes break out over the surface and the edges are crisp.
7. Flip the pancake and cook the other side briefly, about 30 seconds.
8. Add a little oil to the pan before making each new pancake.
9. Sprinkle with shredded coconut.

CHEMIN DE FER D'ORLÉANS BANLIEUE DE PARIS
CARTES D'ABONNEMENT
A PRIX RÉDUITS, HEBDOMADAIRES, MENSUELLES, TRIMESTRIELLES, SEMESTRIELLES, ANNUELLES.

crêpes with lemon curd & fresh berries

yield: about 6 crêpes

ingredients

Lemon Curd Filling:

- 3 large egg yolks
- 6 tbsp. granulated sugar
- zest of ½ lemon
- ¼ cup lemon juice
- 4 tbsp. unsalted butter, cold, cut into pieces

Crêpes:

- 3 large eggs
- ¾ cup water
- 1 tbsp. unsalted butter, melted and cooled
- 1 cup gluten free all-purpose flour
- ¼ cup potato starch
- 1 tsp. salt
- 1 tsp. granulated sugar
- vegetable oil for frying
- 1 cup assorted fresh berries

directions

Lemon Curd Filling:

1. In a small saucepan whisk together yolks, sugar, lemon zest, and lemon juice. Set over medium heat, whisking constantly. Cook for 5-7 minutes or until mixture is thick and lemon colored. Remove saucepan from heat. Add butter, one piece at a time, stirring until consistency is smooth.
2. Transfer mixture to a bowl. Lay a sheet of plastic wrap directly on the surface of the curd to avoid a skin from forming and wrap tightly. Refrigerate until firm and chilled, at least 1 hour.

Crêpes:

1. In a small bowl, blend eggs, water, and butter; set aside. In a separate bowl combine flour, potato starch, salt, and sugar.
2. Slowly whisk the dry ingredients into the wet until smooth. The batter should be thin; if it's too thick, add more water.
3. Heat a small frying pan over medium-high heat without oil for at least 1 minute or until the pan is hot. This will help keep the crêpes from sticking.
4. Add a little oil (about ½ tsp.) and swirl it around the pan.
5. Add about ¼ cup batter (depending on how large or thick you want your crêpes), tilting the pan this way and that to distribute the batter and create a round crêpe.
6. Allow the batter to cook at least 1 minute or until small holes break out over the surface and the edges are crisp.
7. Flip the crêpe and cook the other side briefly. Add about 2 tsp. of lemon curd filling per crêpe and top with assorted fresh berries. Flip over half, as you would an omelet, allowing the lemon filling to disperse.
8. Add a little oil to the pan before making each new crêpe.

Kilkenny, Ireland

let's cook: irish soda corn bread

ingredients:

- 1 cup cornmeal
- 1 cup gluten free all-purpose flour
- 1 tsp. xantham gum
- 1 tsp. baking soda
- ½ tsp. baking powder
- a pinch of salt
- 1 cup milk
- 3 tbsp. olive oil
- 1 tbsp. honey
- butter, preferably Irish butter (optional)

yield: 8 servings

directions:

1. Preheat oven to 375° and grease and flour an 8-inch cake pan.
2. In a large bowl, combine all ingredients with an electric mixer until well blended.
3. Pour into cake pan and bake until toothpick inserted in center comes out clean, about 45 minutes.
4. Serve warm with Irish butter if desired.

lemon ricotta pancakes

yield: 4 servings

ingredients

- 1 ¼ cups gluten free all-purpose flour
- 1 ½ tsp. baking powder
- 1 tsp. salt
- 3 tbsp. granulated sugar or agave nectar
- 3 large eggs
- 1 cup milk
- 1 tsp. pure vanilla extract
- 1 tbsp. lemon zest (from about 2-3 medium lemons)
- ¾ cup whole milk ricotta cheese
- 5 tbsp. unsalted butter, melted and cooled
- butter or cooking spray for frying
- confectioners' sugar and berries or your favorite berry jam

directions

1. Mix all ingredients in a bowl. Batter should be smooth and creamy.
2. Heat a large non-stick frying pan, griddle, or seasoned cast iron skillet over medium heat until hot, about 4 minutes. Test to see if the pan is hot enough by sprinkling a couple of drops of cold water in it: if the water bounces and sputters, the pan is ready to use.
3. Lightly coat the pan's surface with butter or cooking spray, then use a ¼ cup measure to scoop the batter into the pan. Cook until bubbles form on top of the pancakes, about 4-5 minutes. Flip and cook the other side until the bottoms are golden brown, about 1-2 minutes more.
4. Repeat with remaining batter. Top with confectioners' sugar, berries or your jam of choice and serve immediately.

onion lover's spinach scramble

yield: 1-2 servings

ingredients

- 2 large eggs
- salt and freshly ground black pepper to taste
- a pinch of turmeric
- 2 tbsp. olive oil
- 1 large white onion, diced
- 1 tbsp. chopped garlic
- 4 cups chopped fresh spinach

directions

1. Using a fork, mix eggs and season with salt, pepper, and turmeric. Set aside.
2. Heat olive oil in a skillet over medium heat, then add onion and garlic and brown for 5 minutes.
3. Add spinach and cook until soft, about 1 minute.
4. Once spinach is done, pour raw scrambled eggs into pan. Turn off heat and scramble eggs with onions and spinach until cooked to your taste.

These flowers are blooming onions!!

Safed, Israel

shakshuka

(Poached Eggs in a Tomato Sauce)

yield: 3 servings

ingredients

- 3 tbsp. olive oil
- 1 large white onion, diced
- 1 large red bell pepper, deseeded and diced
- 6 garlic cloves, chopped
- 1 tsp. ground cumin
- 1 tsp. turmeric
- a pinch of cayenne pepper (optional)
- 3 cups tomato sauce
- salt and freshly ground black pepper to taste
- 1 ¼ cups crumbled feta cheese
- 6 large eggs
- 1 tbsp. chopped fresh cilantro or parsley
- hot sauce (optional)

directions

1. Preheat oven to 375˚.
2. Heat oil in a large oven-safe skillet over medium-low heat. Add onion and bell pepper. Cook gently until very soft, about 20 minutes. Add garlic and cook until tender, about 1-2 minutes. Stir in cumin, turmeric, and cayenne pepper, if using, and cook an additional minute.
3. Pour in tomato sauce and season with salt and pepper. Simmer until sauce has thickened, about 10 minutes, then stir in crumbled feta.
4. Gently crack eggs into skillet over tomato sauce and top with salt and pepper. Transfer skillet to oven and bake until eggs are cooked to your taste, about 7-10 minutes. Remove from oven and sprinkle with cilantro or parsley. Serve with hot sauce if desired.

Soups & Salads

Quito, Ecuador
The prize goes to the person who can guess how many beans are in this bowl.

4 bean & kale super stew

yield: 6 servings

ingredients

- 3 tbsp. olive oil
- 2 celery stalks, diced
- 2 white onions, diced
- 2 carrots, peeled and diced
- 1 red bell pepper, deseeded, stemmed, and chopped
- 1 yellow bell pepper, deseeded, stemmed, and chopped
- 12 cups water
- 1 (15 oz.) can lentils
- 1 (15 oz.) can chickpeas
- 1 (15 oz.) can navy beans
- 1 (15 oz.) can kidney beans (or any four beans of your choice)
- 2 sweet potatoes, peeled and diced
- 1 cup chopped kale
- 1 cup chopped spinach
- 3-4 whole cloves
- 1 tbsp. chopped fresh parsley
- 1 tsp. peeled, chopped fresh ginger
- 2 tbsp. chopped garlic
- 1 tsp. turmeric
- 1 tsp. chili powder
- 1 tsp. ground cumin
- 1 tsp. curry powder

directions

1. Heat oil in a large soup pot over medium-high heat, then sauté celery, onion and carrots with red and yellow peppers, stirring occasionally, until softened, about 5 minutes. Add water followed by lentils, chickpeas, navy beans, kidney beans, sweet potatoes, kale, spinach, cloves, parsley, ginger, garlic, turmeric, chili powder, cumin, and curry powder and bring to a boil. Reduce heat to medium. Simmer until beans are tender, about 2-3 hours.

beef pho

(Vietnamese Beef Noodle Soup)

yield: 6 servings

ingredients

Stock:

- 12 cups water
- 2 cups beef stock
- 2 lbs. beef bones (optional, but preferred)
- 1 large white onion, halved
- 2 carrots, peeled and cut into chunks
- 2 tbsp. peeled, sliced fresh ginger
- a pinch of salt
- 1 cinnamon stick, about 3-inches long
- 6 whole cloves
- 6 peppercorns
- 6 coriander seeds
- 4 whole star anise

Pho:

- 2 (8 oz.) packages rice noodles
- 8 oz. thick beef steak
- 2 tbsp. gluten free soy sauce
- ½ cup bean sprouts, washed
- 1 large white onion, thinly sliced
- 3 scallions, finely chopped

To season:

- ½ cup fresh cilantro, torn into sprigs
- ½ cup chopped fresh mint
- 1 red chili, deseeded, stemmed, and sliced into rings
- lime wedges

directions

1. To make the stock, pour water into a large pot and add beef stock; add the beef bones as well, if using. Bring to a boil and skim off foaming scum from surface (this should take about 6-8 minutes). Reduce heat to medium-low, partly cover, and simmer for 2 hours, skimming often. Add onion, carrots, ginger, salt, cinnamon stick, cloves, peppercorns, coriander seeds, and whole star anise and simmer another 1 ½ hours, then remove from heat.
2. Drain stock through a fine sieve, then set aside. Discard bones, carrots, onion, and spices. Once cooled, skim fat from stock.
3. While stock is cooking, soak rice noodles in warm water until soft, about 20 minutes. Drain noodles and set aside. Slice steak into paper thin slices and set aside as well.
4. Once stock is ready, pour in soy sauce and bring liquid to a boil, then reduce heat to very low.
5. Pour boiling stock into 6 serving bowls, add drained noodles, then top equally with bean sprouts, raw onion, scallions, and raw steak slices. Season with cilantro, mint, chili, and lime.

Hanoi, Vietnam

Otavalo, Ecuador

I was told to always haggle at the market. This llama told me it would cost $20 to take his picture. I countered with $10 and we settled on $15. Moral of this story: llamas WILL try to rip you off.

black bean & corn salad

yield: 4-6 servings

ingredients

- 1 (15 oz.) can black beans, rinsed and drained
- 1 (15 oz.) can kidney beans, rinsed and drained
- 1 (15 oz.) can lima beans, rinsed and drained
- 8-10 oz. cooked corn, fresh or frozen (thawed if frozen)
- 1 large tomato, chopped
- 1 small red onion, diced
- 1 bunch of scallions, chopped
- 2 tbsp. chopped fresh cilantro
- salt and freshly ground black pepper to taste
- juice of 1 lime or more if desired
- 3 tbsp. olive oil
- 1 medium Hass avocado, diced
- ½ jalapeño, deseeded, stemmed, and chopped (optional)

directions

1. In a large bowl, combine beans, corn, tomato, onion, scallions, cilantro, salt, and pepper. Squeeze in lime juice and stir in oil. Marinate in the refrigerator for 30 minutes. Add avocado and jalapeño, if using, just before serving.

   Tip: To rinse beans, combine all in a strainer or colander and run under cool, flowing water until the water runs clear.

Montmartre, France
A classic view of the famous Eiffel Tower from the hills of Montmartre.

candied fig & goat cheese salad

ÉTAT FRANÇAIS
CONTRIBUTIONS INDIRECTES
FRANCE

yield: 4 servings

ingredients

- 8 fresh figs, pitted and sliced
- 8 fresh apricots, pitted and sliced
- ½ cup crumbled goat cheese
- ¼ cup balsamic vinegar
- ¼ cup maple syrup
- 2 cups mixed baby greens
- ½ cup candied pecans

Tip: To make your own candied pecans, melt 2 tbsp. salted butter over medium-high heat, then add 2 cups pecan halves and toss to coat. Add 4 tbsp. brown sugar and stir until caramelized, about 5 minutes. Spread on wax paper and allow to cool. (Makes 2 cups)

directions

1. Preheat oven to 400˚.
2. Place fig and apricot slices on a baking sheet.
3. Sprinkle with goat cheese and drizzle with vinegar and maple syrup.
4. Roast for 20 minutes.
5. Spoon figs, apricots, and accumulated juices over baby greens.
6. Add candied pecans.
7. Serve immediately.

chestnut soup

yield: 6 servings

ingredients

- light extra-virgin olive or canola oil for sautéing
- 1 large white onion, chopped
- 1 carrot, peeled and chopped
- 2 celery stalks, chopped
- 4 cups vegetable stock
- 2 cups roughly chopped white mushrooms
- 10 oz. peeled, roasted whole chestnuts (packaged is fine)
- 1 cup almond milk
- ¼ cup Marsala wine
- salt and freshly ground black pepper to taste

directions

1. Cover the bottom of a medium soup pot with oil and heat over medium-high heat, then add onion, carrot, and celery and sauté until onion is translucent, about 5 minutes.
2. Add stock, mushrooms, and chestnuts; bring to a boil.
3. Reduce heat and simmer for 30 minutes. Stir in almond milk and wine and heat through.
4. Purée soup using an immersion blender or in batches using a regular blender or food processor.
5. Season with salt and pepper.

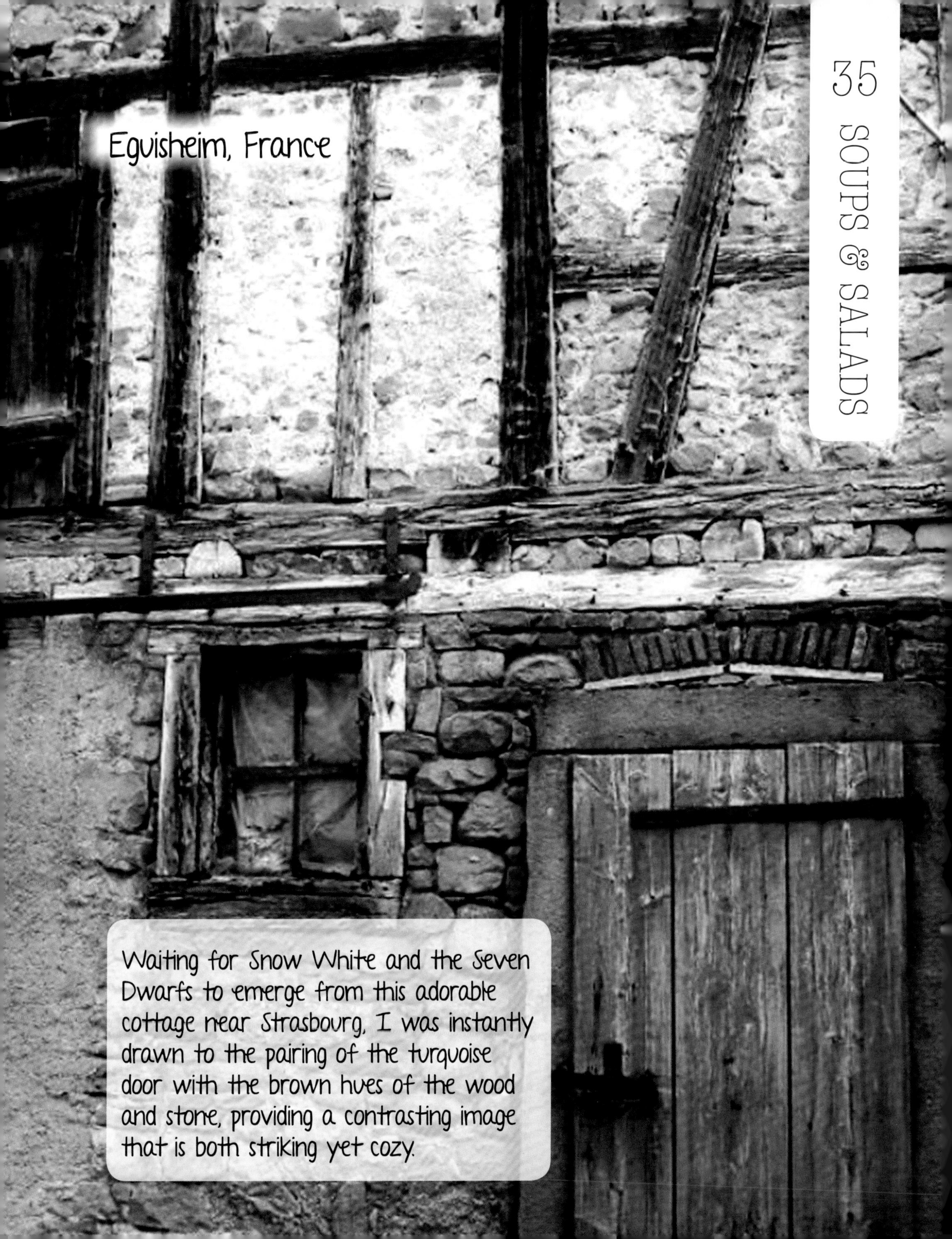

Eguisheim, France

Waiting for Snow White and the Seven Dwarfs to emerge from this adorable cottage near Strasbourg, I was instantly drawn to the pairing of the turquoise door with the brown hues of the wood and stone, providing a contrasting image that is both striking yet cozy.

Ranakpur, India

Carved in exquisite detail from a single marble rock, the Jain Temple, constructed in 1473 C.E. easily puts modern architecture to shame.

curried quinoa salad with mint raita

yield: 4 servings

ingredients

- 1 tsp. olive oil
- 2 tsp. curry powder
- 1 garlic clove, chopped
- 1 cup uncooked quinoa, rinsed
- 2 cups water
- ¾ tsp. salt
- 1 ripe mango, peeled and diced
- 3 tbsp. plain craisins or gluten free dried cranberries
- 6 oz. plain yogurt
- 2 tsp. chopped fresh mint
- ½ cup diced celery
- ¼ cup thinly sliced scallions
- 3 tbsp. chopped fresh cilantro or parsley
- 1 cup fresh baby spinach

directions

1. Heat oil in a medium saucepan over medium-high heat.
2. Stirring constantly, add curry powder and garlic to pan and cook until lightly browned and fragrant, about 30 seconds.
3. Add quinoa and water; bring to a boil. Once boiling, cover, reduce heat, and simmer, until quinoa is tender, about 15 minutes.
4. Remove from heat, stir in salt, and let cool completely.
5. Add mango and craisins or dried cranberries to cooled quinoa and gently toss.
6. To create raita sauce, combine yogurt and mint in a small bowl and stir well.
7. In a salad bowl, combine celery, scallions, cilantro or parsley, and spinach.
8. Add quinoa mixture to spinach mix and drizzle with raita sauce.

Sa Pa, Vietnam

curried yam soup

yield: 4 servings

ingredients

- 3 medium yams, unpeeled and quartered
- 4 tbsp. olive oil, divided
- salt to taste
- 1 large white onion, chopped
- 2 celery stalks, chopped
- 2 garlic cloves, finely chopped
- 1 tbsp. garam masala
- 1 tsp. curry powder
- 5 cups chicken or vegetable stock
- 1 cup coconut milk
- ½ cup water

directions

1. Preheat oven to 400˚.
2. Place yams on a baking sheet and drizzle with 2 tbsp. oil. Season with salt, then bake until tender, about 1 hour. Remove from oven and set aside to cool.
3. Meanwhile, in a large saucepan, heat the remaining 2 tbsp. oil over medium-high heat. Sauté onion and celery, stirring frequently, until onion is translucent, about 5 minutes. Add garlic and sauté another 30 seconds.
4. Add garam masala and curry powder. Continue to sauté, stirring constantly with a wooden spoon, for 30 seconds, then remove saucepan from heat.
5. Scoop flesh out of yams and discard skins. Place yam pulp into the saucepan and stir well to coat yams with spices. Add stock and bring to a boil. Once boiling, reduce heat to medium-low and cover. Simmer soup for 15 minutes, then remove from heat and let cool.
6. Purée soup using an immersion blender or in batches, using a regular blender or food processor, until smooth and creamy. Place soup back into saucepan over medium heat and add coconut milk and water. Simmer for 5 minutes.

A beautiful field of quinoa in Ecuador.

feta cheese & quinoa salad

yield: 4 servings

ingredients

- 2 cups vegetable stock
- 1 cup uncooked quinoa, rinsed
- 2 cups chopped fresh Italian parsley
- 1 cup pitted, sliced Kalamata olives
- 1 cup halved cherry tomatoes
- 1 medium, peeled, deseeded cucumber, diced
- 1 small red onion, chopped
- ½ cup crumbled feta cheese
- 3 tbsp. extra-virgin olive oil
- 2 tbsp. balsamic vinegar
- juice of 1 lemon or more if desired
- salt and freshly ground black pepper to taste

directions

1. Bring vegetable stock to a boil. Once boiling, pour in quinoa and simmer, covered, for 20 minutes, stirring occasionally.
2. Transfer quinoa to a large bowl. Add parsley, olives, tomatoes, cucumber, onion, and feta cheese.
3. Pour oil, vinegar, lemon juice, salt, and pepper over ingredients and mix well.

Kinsale, Ireland

irish blue potato beef stew

yield: 4-6 servings

ingredients

- 2 large white onions, diced
- 2 tbsp. chopped garlic
- 3 tbsp. olive oil
- 1 lb. beef chuck cubes
- 1 tsp. paprika
- 1 carrot, diced
- 1 turnip, diced
- 1 parsnip, diced
- 4-5 blue potatoes, diced
- 4 cups beef stock
- 1 cup sauerkraut
- ¼ cup sauerkraut brine
- ½ cup dry red wine
- 4 thyme sprigs
- 1 tbsp. chopped fresh marjoram or 1 tsp. dried marjoram (optional)

directions

1. Sauté onions and garlic in oil for 5 minutes, stirring occasionally. Add beef, sprinkle with paprika, and cook, tossing meat chunks occasionally, until brown, about 6-8 minutes.
2. Add carrot, turnip, parsnip, potatoes, stock, sauerkraut, brine, wine, thyme, and marjoram, if using.
3. Bring to a boil, then reduce heat and simmer until potatoes are soft, about 1 hour.

San Gimiginano, Italy

italian wedding soup

yield: 8 servings

ingredients

Meatballs:

- 1 bunch of scallions, chopped
- ⅓ cup chopped fresh Italian parsley
- 1 large egg
- 1 tsp. minced garlic
- 1 tsp. salt
- freshly ground black pepper to taste
- 1 tbsp. gluten free panko or bread crumbs
- 1 lb. ground beef

Soup:

- 12 cups chicken stock
- 4 cups spinach
- salt and freshly ground black pepper to taste
- 1 cup quinoa rinsed and prepared according to package directions

directions

Meatballs:

1. Stir scallions, parsley, egg, garlic, salt, pepper, and panko or bread crumbs in a large bowl to blend, then stir in beef. Shape meat mixture into 1-inch round meatballs and place on a baking sheet.

Soup:

1. Bring stock to a boil in a large pot over medium-high heat. Add meatballs and spinach. Simmer until meatballs are cooked and spinach is tender, about 8 minutes.
2. Season soup with salt and pepper.
3. Divide soup into serving bowls then add equal amounts of quinoa to each.

mandarin orange chicken salad

yield: 4 servings

ingredients

Chicken:

- salt and freshly ground black pepper to taste
- 1 ½ tsp. paprika
- ⅛ tsp. garlic powder
- ⅛ tsp. onion powder
- 1 lb. boneless, skinless chicken breasts, cut into strips
- 2 tbsp. olive oil

Dressing:

- 4 tbsp. extra-virgin olive oil
- 2 tbsp. mandarin orange liquid
- 2 tbsp. rice wine vinegar
- 1 ½ tbsp. gluten free soy sauce
- 1 tbsp. granulated sugar or agave nectar
- 2 tsp. toasted sesame oil
- ¼ tsp. yellow mustard
- ⅛ tsp. ground ginger
- ¼ tsp. garlic powder

Salad Ingredients:

- 3-5 cups mixed baby greens
- 1-2 cups fresh mint leaves
- 1 (16 oz.) can mandarin oranges, liquid drained and set aside
- ½ cup candied pecans (found on pg. 33)
- 2 avocados, cubed

directions

1. In a large bowl, combine salt, pepper, paprika, garlic powder, and onion powder to create a spice mixture for the chicken.
2. Coat chicken breasts lightly in olive oil. Rub spice mixture onto both sides of chicken breasts, then return chicken to bowl.
3. Refrigerate chicken for at least 30 minutes to absorb flavors.
4. To cook the chicken, you can either grill it over high heat for about 15 minutes, flipping frequently, or pan-fry it over medium heat for about 5 minutes per side.
5. Mix dressing and toss with baby greens, mint, mandarin oranges, candied pecans, avocados, and chicken. Serve immediately.

Chiang Mai, Thailand

moroccan mint beet salad

yield: 4-6 servings

ingredients

- 6 medium beets (3 gold, 3 red)
- 4 scallions, chopped
- 2 cups roughly chopped fresh mint
- ¼ cup balsamic vinegar
- 2 tbsp. extra-virgin olive oil
- 2 tsp. granulated sugar or agave nectar
- juice of 1 lime
- 1 tsp. ground cumin

directions

1. Rinse and trim beets. Place in a pot of cold water and bring to a boil. Reduce heat to a simmer and cook until fork tender, about 1 hour.
2. Remove beets from water and allow to cool, then peel and dice into bite-sized pieces.
3. Add scallions and mint to beets.
4. In a separate bowl, mix together vinegar, oil, sugar or agave nectar, lime juice, and cumin.
5. Pour over beets, scallions, and mint and toss ingredients to coat evenly.
6. Serve chilled.

Bangkok, Thailand

pepper steak salad

yield: 4 servings

ingredients

- 2 tbsp. olive oil
- 1 medium yellow onion, chopped
- 2 assorted bell peppers, deseeded, stemmed, and sliced into thin strips
- 2 garlic cloves, minced
- ⅓ cup gluten free soy sauce
- 3 tbsp. toasted sesame oil
- 1 tbsp. honey or agave nectar
- 1 ½ lbs. chuck, hanger, rib, or skirt steak, cut into thin strips
- 8 cups fresh spinach leaves

directions

1. Heat olive oil in a skillet over medium heat. Cook onion, bell peppers, and garlic, stirring frequently, until tender but still crispy, about 3-4 minutes. Remove vegetables from skillet and set aside.
2. Heat the skillet over medium-high heat. Pour soy sauce, toasted sesame oil, and honey or agave nectar into the pan, then add steak strips. Cook steak, stirring frequently, for about 10 minutes. Stir in cooked vegetables and cook another 10-15 minutes.
3. Once steak is finished cooking, pour all contents of pan including sauce over spinach. Toss and serve immediately.

Ardith Mae
FARMSTEAD GOAT CHEESE

Fresh Chevre $8
- Lightly Salted w/Sea Salt

Garic Scape + Black Pepper Chevre $9

Herb Chevre $6
- fresh Chev coated in herbs

FETA

Brine

pomegranate & goat cheese salad

yield: 4 servings

ingredients

- 8 cups mixed baby greens
- ¼ cup pomegranate seeds
- 1 small red onion, chopped
- ¼ cup crumbled goat cheese
- ¼ cup walnuts

Dressing:

- 3 tbsp. maple syrup
- 2 tbsp. balsamic vinegar
- 2 tbsp. extra-virgin olive oil

directions

1. In a large bowl, toss greens, pomegranate seeds, onion, goat cheese, and walnuts.
2. In a separate, small bowl, whisk together maple syrup, vinegar, and oil. Drizzle over salad, toss ingredients, and serve immediately.

sweet potato leek soup

yield: 6 servings

ingredients

- 2 tbsp. extra-virgin olive oil
- 4 leeks, trimmed
- 1 celery stalk, chopped
- 1 small yellow onion, diced
- 2 garlic cloves, minced
- 8 cups chicken or vegetable stock
- 1 cup Riesling or other white wine
- 2 large sweet potatoes, peeled and quartered
- 1 tsp. salt
- ½ tsp. freshly ground black pepper
- 1 ½ tsp. chopped fresh thyme or ½ tsp. dried thyme
- 2 tsp. chopped fresh parsley
- 2 tsp. chopped fresh dill
- 2 tsp. chopped fresh tarragon
- 1 cup soymilk
- thyme sprigs

directions

1. Heat oil in a large pan, then add leeks, celery, onion, and garlic. Sauté over medium heat, stirring occasionally, until vegetables are soft, about 6 minutes.
2. Stir in stock, wine, potatoes, salt, pepper, and thyme; bring to a boil.
3. Reduce heat and simmer over medium heat until potatoes are soft, about 20-30 minutes.
4. Add parsley, dill, and tarragon and bring soup to a light simmer, stirring occasionally.
5. Remove soup from heat and add soymilk. Blend with an immersion blender. Garnish with thyme sprigs.

Obernai Wine Countries, France (bordering France and Germany)
Luckily for more reasons than one, I was not at the wheel while driving through the winding roads of this breathtaking Alsatian wine country.

THAILAND
ลก 194
กรุงเทพมหานคร

thai beef salad

yield: 6 servings

ingredients

- 1 lb. London broil
- ½ cup gluten free soy sauce
- 3 heads green and red romaine lettuce, washed, dried, and coarsely cut
- 1 red onion, thinly sliced
- 2 cups grape tomatoes, halved
- 3 assorted bell peppers, deseeded, stemmed, and thinly sliced
- ¼ cup thinly sliced white mushrooms

Dressing:

- ⅓ cup granulated sugar or agave nectar
- ¾ cup extra-virgin olive oil
- ⅓ cup white vinegar
- 2 tsp. gluten free soy sauce

directions

1. Set oven to broil.
2. Place beef in a broiler pan. Pour soy sauce over beef and broil for 10 minutes, turning once halfway through cooking time.
3. Transfer meat to a cutting board. Let cool for about 30 minutes, then thinly slice steak strips against the grain.
3. Place the lettuce, onion, tomatoes, bell peppers, mushrooms and beef in a large bowl.
4. Whisk together dressing ingredients, pour over salad, and toss.

Sides

Tam Kok, Vietnam

let's cook: baby bok choy with garlic & ginger

ingredients:

- 3 heads baby bok choy, stalks and leaves
- 3 tbsp. olive oil
- 2 tbsp. sesame oil
- 1 tsp. peeled, minced fresh ginger

yield: 6 servings

- ¼ - ½ tsp. red chili flakes
- 2 garlic cloves, thinly sliced
- 1 scallion, thinly sliced
- 3 tbsp. gluten free soy sauce

directions:

1. Trim ends from bok choy and discard, then chop and rinse stalks and leaves in a bowl of water.
2. Heat oils in a skillet over medium heat. Add ginger, chili flakes, garlic, and scallion and cook for about 4 minutes, stirring to avoid sticking.
3. Turn off heat. Add bok choy and soy sauce and steam until tender but still al dente, about 2-4 minutes.

Colorful Sunday market in Pushkar, India

bhinidi masala

(Stir Fried Curried Okra)

yield: 4 servings

ingredients

- 2 tbsp. coconut or extra-virgin olive oil, divided
- 2 lbs. okra, washed, dried, ends trimmed, and cut into 1-inch pieces
- 1 tsp. cumin seeds
- 1 large white onion, finely chopped
- ½ tsp. green chili paste
- 1 tbsp. peeled, chopped fresh ginger
- 5 garlic cloves, chopped
- ¾ tsp. chili powder
- ¾ tsp. ground coriander
- ¼ tsp. turmeric
- 1 medium tomato, finely chopped
- salt to taste
- 1 tsp. garam masala
- cooked rice (optional)

directions

1. Heat 1 tbsp. oil in a medium pot, add okra, and sauté over medium-low heat for 8 minutes. Remove from pot and set aside.
2. In the same pot, add the 1 tbsp. remaining oil. Once hot, add cumin seeds and toast until fragrant, about 2-3 minutes. Add onion and green chili paste and sauté for 4 minutes, then add ginger and garlic and sauté for 3 minutes. Stir in chili powder, coriander, and turmeric.
3. Add tomato, cover, and cook for 6-7 minutes over medium-low heat.
4. Add okra and mix well. Cook uncovered for 10 minutes. Add salt and garam masala and stir. Turn off heat. Serve warm with rice if desired.

Otovalo, Ecuador
The beauty of the clothing and culture at this colorful animal market was astounding!

bocaditos de papa

(Potato - Cheese Fritters)

yield: 12 fritters

ingredients

- 1 lb. russet potatoes, peeled and quartered
- 1 cup shredded pepper jack or cheddar cheese
- 2 tbsp. shredded Parmesan cheese
- 3 large eggs, lightly beaten
- 1 tbsp. chopped fresh cilantro
- ½ tsp. salt
- ½ tsp. ground cumin
- ¼ tsp. cayenne pepper
- canola oil for deep frying
- salsa (optional)

directions

1. In a large saucepan, place potatoes in enough salted water to cover. Bring to a boil, then reduce heat. Simmer, covered, for 15-20 minutes or until potatoes are tender, then drain.
2. In a large bowl, mash potatoes with a potato masher until smooth. Fold in cheeses, eggs, cilantro, salt, cumin, and cayenne pepper. Shape mixture into twelve, 3-inch diameter patties. If desired, cover and chill for up to 24 hours before cooking.
3. In a large skillet, heat 1-inch of oil to 375˚. Add potato patties, three or four at a time and fry, about 2 minutes or until golden brown, turning once halfway through cooking time. Drain on paper towels. Serve hot and top with salsa if desired.

Tam Kok, Vietnam

ginger brown rice

yield: 4 servings

ingredients

- 1 cup short grain brown rice
- 4 tbsp. olive oil
- 1 large white onion, diced
- 2 garlic cloves, minced
- 1 yellow bell pepper, deseeded, stemmed, and diced
- 1 red bell pepper, deseeded, stemmed, and diced
- 1 orange bell pepper, deseeded, stemmed, and diced
- 1 green zucchini, diced
- 1 yellow squash, diced
- 1 tsp. peeled, minced fresh ginger
- 2 tsp. black sesame seeds

directions

1. Prepare rice according to the directions on the package.
2. Heat oil in a skillet over medium-high heat and sauté onion and garlic until onion is translucent and garlic is golden brown, about 5 minutes. Add peppers, zucchini, squash, and ginger and cook until soft, about 5-7 minutes. Remove from heat, then add prepared rice and sesame seeds to skillet. Toss until evenly dispersed.

indian spiced roasted chickpeas

yield: 4 servings

ingredients

- 2 tbsp. olive oil
- 2 tbsp. canola oil
- 1 tbsp. Earth Balance Buttery Spread
- 1 (15 oz.) can chickpeas, rinsed and drained
- ½ tsp. ground cumin
- ¼ tsp. garlic powder
- ½ tsp. ground coriander
- ½ tsp. paprika
- ½ tsp. cayenne pepper
- kosher salt and cracked black pepper to taste

directions

1. Place oils and Earth Balance in a large sauté pan over medium heat.
2. When the Earth Balance spread has melted, add chickpeas and toss to coat them completely.
3. Add all spices and toss chickpeas again to coat with spice mixture.
4. Sauté chickpeas over medium-low heat until they begin to pop, about 10 minutes.

Sonamarg, India

I had to do a double take when I saw two trees walking towards me while hiking in the Himalayan Mountains. Turns out they were not trees, but two women gathering leaves in anticipation of the winter months during which greenery (food for their sheep and cattle) is scarce.

Kinsale, Ireland

irish garlic brussels sprouts

yield: 4 servings

ingredients

- 5 tbsp. olive oil
- garlic powder, salt, and freshly ground black pepper to taste
- 2 cups Brussels sprouts, halved

directions

1. Preheat oven to 400°.
2. Rub oil, a generous amount of garlic powder, salt and pepper on Brussels sprouts.
3. Pour mixture into a 9x13 pan.
4. Roast, uncovered, until golden brown, about 45 minutes, tossing occasionally.

layered ratatouille

yield: 6-8 servings

ingredients

- cooking spray
- 5-6 Campari or other small tomatoes, sliced into ¼-inch circles
- ¼ cup olive oil
- 2 tbsp. chopped fresh herbs de Provence (fresh oregano, basil, thyme, and parsley)
- salt and freshly ground black pepper to taste
- 18 garlic cloves, chopped
- 2 Japanese eggplants, sliced into ¼-inch circles
- 4 zucchinis, sliced into ¼-inch circles
- 1 cup tomato sauce

directions

1. Preheat oven to 350° and spray a 9x13 baking dish with cooking spray.
2. Place tomatoes in the prepared dish and drizzle with some of the oil, herbs, salt, pepper, and garlic.
3. Repeat with eggplant and then zucchini, adding oil and herbs.
4. Pour tomato sauce over vegetables.
5. Cover the dish and bake for 45 minutes.
6. When fully baked, carefully pour out excess liquid.

I passed this French pastoral scenery while riding my bike in Giverny on the way to see Monet!

DATE No. 23/100

lemon jerra rice

yield: 4 servings

ingredients

- 1 ½ cups uncooked white Indian Basmati rice
- 3 cups water
- salt to taste
- 2-4 tbsp. cumin seeds
- 2 tbsp. light extra-virgin olive or canola oil, divided
- grated zest of 2 lemons
- 2 tbsp. olive oil
- 2 tbsp. Earth Balance Buttery Spread
- freshly ground black pepper to taste
- chopped fresh cilantro or parsley

directions

1. Wash basmati rice well in running water, then place washed rice in a pot.
2. Add water and salt to rice, bring to a boil, cover pot, and cook until rice is done, about 20 minutes.
3. Once rice is cooked, transfer it to a bowl. (don't mix or it gets gummy!)
4. In another pan, toast cumin seeds in 1 tbsp. oil until fragrant, about 1 minute. The seeds will sputter and sizzle to show they are done.
5. Add toasted cumin seeds to rice bowl, then add lemon zest, the remaining 1 tbsp. oil, Earth Balance, salt, and pepper.
6. Fluff with a fork. Do not over mix or rice will become mushy.
7. Garnish with cilantro or parsley.

Rajasthan, India
Taking a break from picking rice to pose for a pretty picture.

AVIVA
Kanoff '13
By E Suwarno
Bali

maple ginger roasted sweet potatoes

yield: 6 servings

ingredients

- 4 large sweet potatoes, unpeeled and diced
- 3 tbsp. olive oil
- 2 tbsp. peeled, chopped fresh ginger
- 3 tbsp. maple syrup
- a pinch of ground cinnamon
- a pinch of nutmeg

directions

1. Preheat oven to 400°.
2. Mix all ingredients in a large bowl until sweet potatoes are fully coated, then place on a roasting pan and bake until sweet potatoes are soft, about 35-40 minutes, tossing occasionally. Serve immediately.

Walking the streets of Ecuador's capital, Quito.

mexican street corn

yield: 4 servings

ingredients

- 4 large ears of corn
- 4 tbsp. butter, melted
- sea or kosher salt and freshly ground black pepper to taste
- ½ cup mayonnaise
- 1 ½ cups crumbled queso fresco or feta cheese
- 2 tbsp. grated Parmesan cheese
- 4 tbsp. minced fresh cilantro (optional)
- 4 tsp. chili powder
- lime wedges (optional)

directions

1. Preheat oven to 400° or prepare grill. Brush corn with butter and sprinkle with salt and pepper. If roasting, place corn on a baking sheet to cook. Roast or grill for 20-25 minutes, turning once halfway through cooking time.
2. While corn is still hot, working with one ear of corn at a time, brush with mayonnaise, sprinkle with cheeses, cilantro, if using, and chili powder, pressing it onto the corn to help it stick. Sprinkle with additional salt and pepper. Serve with lime wedges if desired.

nutty corn pancakes

yield: 4 servings

ingredients

- 2 large ears of corn
- 1 cup roasted, shelled peanuts
- 3 scallions, chopped
- 2 tsp. peeled, grated fresh ginger
- 1 garlic clove, crushed
- 1 tsp. ground cumin
- 1 large egg, lightly beaten
- ¼ cup rice flour
- ½ cup peanut oil

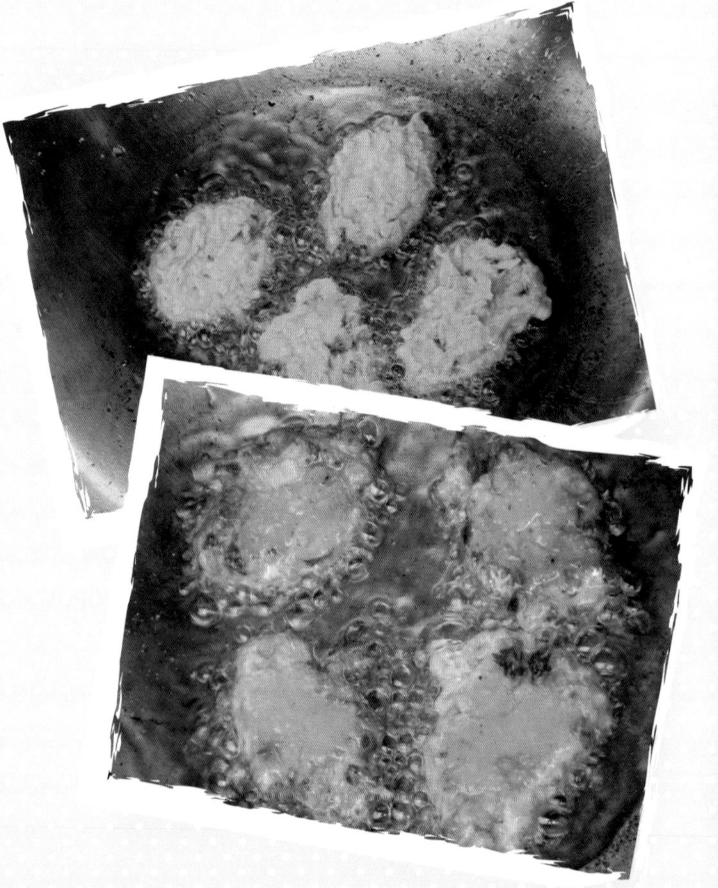

directions

1. Remove kernels from corncobs with a sharp knife, then place kernels in a food processor along with peanuts, scallions, ginger, garlic, and cumin and process until finely chopped and slightly mushy; transfer to a bowl.
2. Add egg and rice flour; mix well.
3. Heat oil in a large skillet over medium heat. Spoon tablespoons of the mixture into the skillet and flatten with the back of the spoon. Cook until golden brown on both sides, about 2 minutes per side. Drain on paper towels and repeat with remaining mixture. Serve hot.

Bali, Indonesia

plantain chips

yield: 6 servings

ingredients

- 2 large green plantains
- 2 tbsp. olive oil
- ½ tsp. salt
- 1 tsp. chili powder
- ½ tsp. ground cumin
- ⅛ tsp. cayenne pepper

Tip: Chips are best eaten immediately, but will keep for about a day.

directions

1. Preheat oven to 400°.
2. Remove plantain peels with a knife then thinly slice the flesh.
3. In a bowl, toss plantain slices with oil, salt, and all spices. Spread in a single layer on a baking sheet.
4. Bake for 15-17 minutes, turning slices once halfway through cooking time. Watch closely after turning so as not to burn.

Quito, Ecuador
Plantains anyone? No?
Okay I'll just take a nap.

This glamorous street sweeper in Pushkar, India is probably fancier than I will ever be in my lifetime.

saffron rice

yield: 6 servings

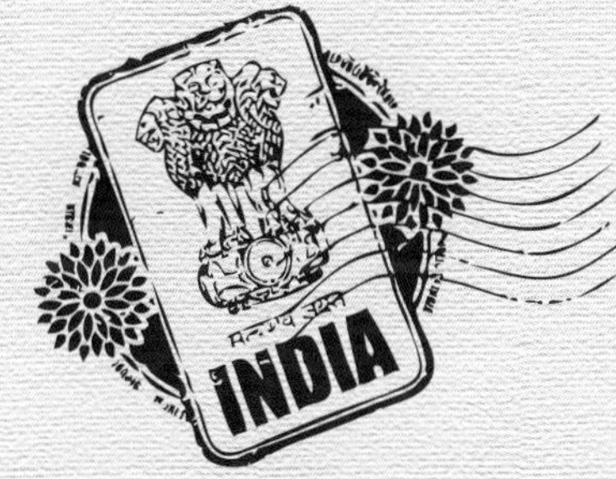

ingredients

- 3-4 saffron threads
- 2 cups boiling water, divided
- 2 tbsp. butter
- 1 cup uncooked long-grain white rice, not rinsed
- 1 tsp. salt

directions

1. Steep the saffron in a ½ cup boiling water.
2. In a skillet that can be tightly covered, melt butter over medium-high heat. Stir in the rice and salt. Cook, stirring constantly, until rice begins to absorb the butter and becomes opaque, but do not brown the rice.
3. Quickly pour in the remaining 1 ½ cups boiling water along with the saffron water. Cover immediately, reduce heat to low, and cook until all liquid is absorbed, about 20 minutes. For best results, do not remove lid while rice is cooking.

Hanoi, Vietnam

sesame garlic string beans

yield: 4 servings

ingredients

- 3 tbsp. toasted sesame oil
- 6 garlic cloves, thinly sliced
- 1 lb. fresh green beans, trimmed
- 3 tbsp. gluten free soy sauce
- 2 tbsp. sesame seeds

directions

1. Heat oil in a wok or large skillet over medium-high heat. Stir in garlic and cook until edges begin to brown, about 20 seconds. Add green beans and cook, stirring frequently, until green beans begin to soften, about 5 minutes. Stir in soy sauce. Continue cooking and stirring for several minutes until green beans have attained desired degree of tenderness. Sprinkle with sesame seeds and serve.

spanish quinoa with sausages

yield: 4 servings

ingredients

- 1 cup quinoa, rinsed
- 4 tbsp. extra-virgin olive oil
- 1 large white onion, chopped
- 1 red bell pepper, deseeded, stemmed, and diced
- 1 yellow bell pepper, deseeded, stemmed, and diced
- 1 orange bell pepper, deseeded, stemmed, and diced
- 12 oz. of your favorite pre-cooked sausage, sliced into ½-inch rounds
- salt, freshly ground black pepper, and garlic powder to taste

directions

1. Prepare quinoa according to the directions on the package.
2. Heat oil in a large skillet, then sauté onion over medium-high heat until translucent, about 5 minutes.
3. Add peppers and cook until soft, about 5 minutes, then add sausages and cook 2 minutes.
4. Turn off heat and season with salt, pepper, and garlic powder.
5. Combine pepper and sausage mixture with cooked quinoa and serve warm.

Málaga, Spain

Fresh Daikons at the market in Pushkar, India

spicy daikon radish fries

yield: 6 servings

ingredients

- ½ cup olive oil
- 1 tbsp. turmeric
- 1 tbsp. ground cumin
- 1 tbsp. ground cardamom
- 1 tbsp. curry powder
- 1 tbsp. minced garlic
- 1 tsp. ground dried fennel
- a pinch of red pepper flakes or more if desired
- salt and freshly ground black pepper to taste
- 2 lbs. daikon radishes, peeled and sliced into "fries"

directions

1. Preheat oven to 450˚.
2. Mix oil and spices together.
3. Pour spice mixture over radishes and mix well until radishes are completely covered.
4. Disperse fries evenly onto a baking sheet.
5. Roast for 15-20 minutes on each side.

A colorful traditional tapestry at the Otavalo Craft Market in Ecuador.

spinach & quinoa fritters

yield: 4 servings

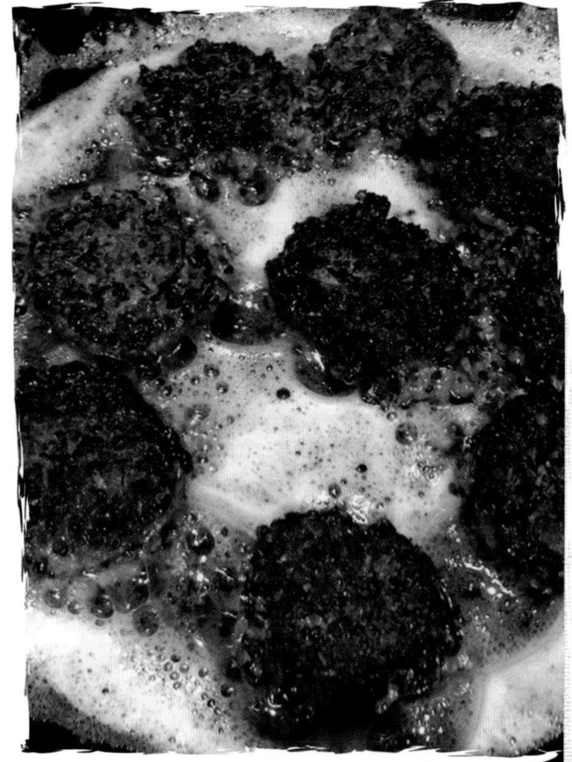

ingredients

- 1 cup quinoa, rinsed
- 1 large white onion, diced
- 2 tbsp. extra-virgin olive oil, plus more for frying
- 2 cups diced fresh mushrooms
- 2 cups chopped spinach
- salt, freshly ground black pepper, and garlic powder to taste
- 3 large eggs
- ¼ cup gluten free panko or bread crumbs
- 2 tbsp. shredded cheddar cheese (optional)

directions

1. Prepare quinoa according to the directions on the package.
2. In a large frying pan, sauté onion in 2 tbsp. oil over medium-high heat until translucent, about 5 minutes.
3. Add mushrooms and spinach and sauté for 3 minutes or until fully cooked.
4. Remove pan from heat. Add quinoa to spinach, mushrooms, and onion mixture and mix ingredients.
5. Season with salt, pepper, and garlic powder.
6. Transfer to a large mixing bowl and combine with eggs, panko or bread crumbs, and cheese, if using.
7. Heat oil in a frying pan. Once oil is sizzling, cooking four pieces at a time, spoon 1 tbsp. of mixture into the frying pan. Cook until golden, about 3 minutes on each side. Remove from pan and drain on paper towels.

C 3944

veggie pakoras

yield: 6 servings

ingredients

- 1 cup chickpea flour
- 1 tsp. salt
- 1 tsp. turmeric
- 1 tsp. ground cumin
- ½ tsp. freshly ground black pepper
- ½ tsp. chili powder
- ½ tsp. garam masala
- 4 garlic cloves, minced
- ¾ cup water
- 4 cups canola oil for frying
- ½ head cauliflower, cut into florets
- 1 medium yellow onion, diced

directions

1. Sift chickpea flour into a medium bowl. Mix in salt, turmeric, cumin, pepper, chili powder, garam masala, and garlic.
2. Create a hole in the center of the flour mixture. Gradually pour water into the hole and mix to form a thick, smooth batter.
3. Heat oil over medium-high heat in a large, heavy saucepan until the oil is hot enough to make a bread crumb sizzle.
4. Place cauliflower and onion in the batter, mix well, and fry batter by the tablespoonful in small batches until golden brown, about 4-5 minutes. Drain on paper towels before serving.

Jaipur, India
These popular Veggie Pakoras are one of India's iconic street foods. Notice the motorbikes in the background. Car exhaust is the secret ingredient so if yours' don't taste just right take them out for a spin!

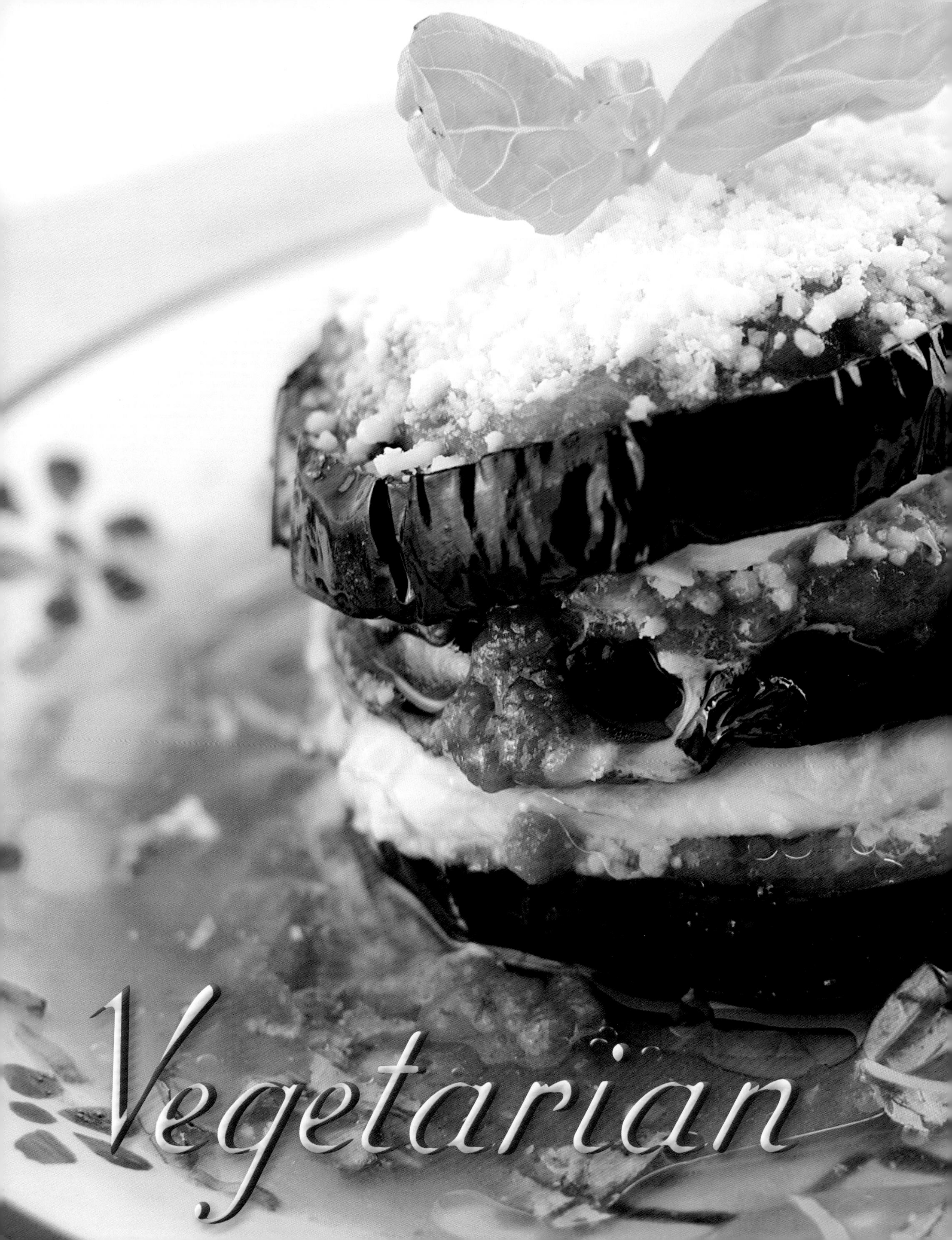

Vegetarian

Rajasthan, India

aloo gobi

(Potato & Cauliflower Curry)

yield: 4-6 servings

ingredients

- 4 tbsp. olive oil
- 1 large white onion, diced
- 2 tbsp. minced garlic
- 2 tbsp. peeled, minced fresh ginger
- 2 large tomatoes, diced
- 2 tsp. turmeric
- 2 tsp. garam masala
- 1 tsp. cumin seeds
- 1 tsp. salt
- 1 bunch of fresh cilantro or parsley, chopped, plus more for garnish if desired
- 1 green chili, deseeded, stemmed, and chopped into small pieces or 1 tsp. chili powder
- 3 large all-purpose potatoes, peeled and diced into medium pieces
- 1 large cauliflower, leaves removed and cut into small florets
- ¼ cup water

directions

1. Heat oil in a large saucepan over medium-high heat.
2. Sauté onion, garlic, and ginger for 3-5 minutes.
3. Add tomatoes, turmeric, garam masala, cumin seeds, salt, cilantro or parsley, and chili or chili powder; cook for 5 minutes then remove from heat.
4. Place potatoes and cauliflower florets in a separate pot. Add water and bring to a boil. Cover pot and steam potatoes and cauliflower until tender, about 20 minutes. Strain potatoes and cauliflower, then add them to the sauce and mix well. Garnish with additional cilantro or parsley if desired.

Amritsar, India
The Golden Temple. Yeah it's real! Properly named, Darbar Harmandir Sahib, it is the holiest place for Sikhs the world over.

bhurtha

(Curried Roasted Eggplant)

yield: 4-6 servings

ingredients

- 2-3 large eggplants, cut into ½-inch thick rounds
- ¼ cup vegetable oil, divided
- 1 tsp. cumin seeds
- 2 medium yellow onions, sliced
- 1 tbsp. peeled, chopped fresh ginger
- 2 garlic cloves, minced
- 2 tbsp. tomato paste
- 1 tsp. turmeric
- 1 tsp. ground cumin
- ½ tsp. cayenne pepper
- salt and freshly ground black pepper to taste
- ½ cup chopped fresh cilantro

directions

1. Set oven to broil.
2. Coat eggplant slices evenly using about 2 tbsp. oil. Disperse eggplant slices onto a greased baking sheet. Place under broiler for about 20 minutes, turning eggplant slices occasionally to prevent burning.
3. Meanwhile, heat the remaining 2 tbsp. oil in a large skillet, wok, or pot over medium high heat. Add cumin seeds and let them crackle for a few seconds and turn golden.
4. Add onion, ginger, and garlic, then cook and stir until tender.
5. Stir in tomato paste and season with turmeric, cumin, cayenne pepper, salt, pepper, and cilantro.
6. Add broiled eggplant slices to skillet and cook, stirring occasionally, for 10-15 minutes.

butternut squash gnocchi

yield: 2 servings

ingredients

- 1 medium butternut squash, peeled and cubed
- 1 large egg
- ¾ tsp. salt
- 1 ½ cups all-purpose gluten free flour, plus more for hands and work surface
- 3 tbsp. butter
- ¼ cup fresh sage leaves
- sea salt to taste
- Parmesan cheese, grated (optional)

directions

1. Boil butternut squash in 4 cups water until soft, then strain.
2. Set a large pot of water to boil. In a medium-sized bowl, combine butternut squash, egg, and salt. Add flour in 3-4 separate additions, stirring to combine after each addition. Continue adding flour until dough is firm enough to handle, but still somewhat sticky.
3. With floured hands, pinch off about a quarter of the dough. Roll between palms and on floured work surface to make a 1-inch thick rope. Cut rope into bite-sized pieces. Repeat with remaining dough.
4. Drop gnocchi into boiling water and cook until they rise to the surface, about 5 minutes. Meanwhile, melt butter in a large, heavy saucepan. Add sage leaves and cook, swirling frequently, until butter browns. Set aside.
5. Drain gnocchi on paper towels, then add to brown butter and toss. Sprinkle with sea salt and Parmesan cheese if desired.

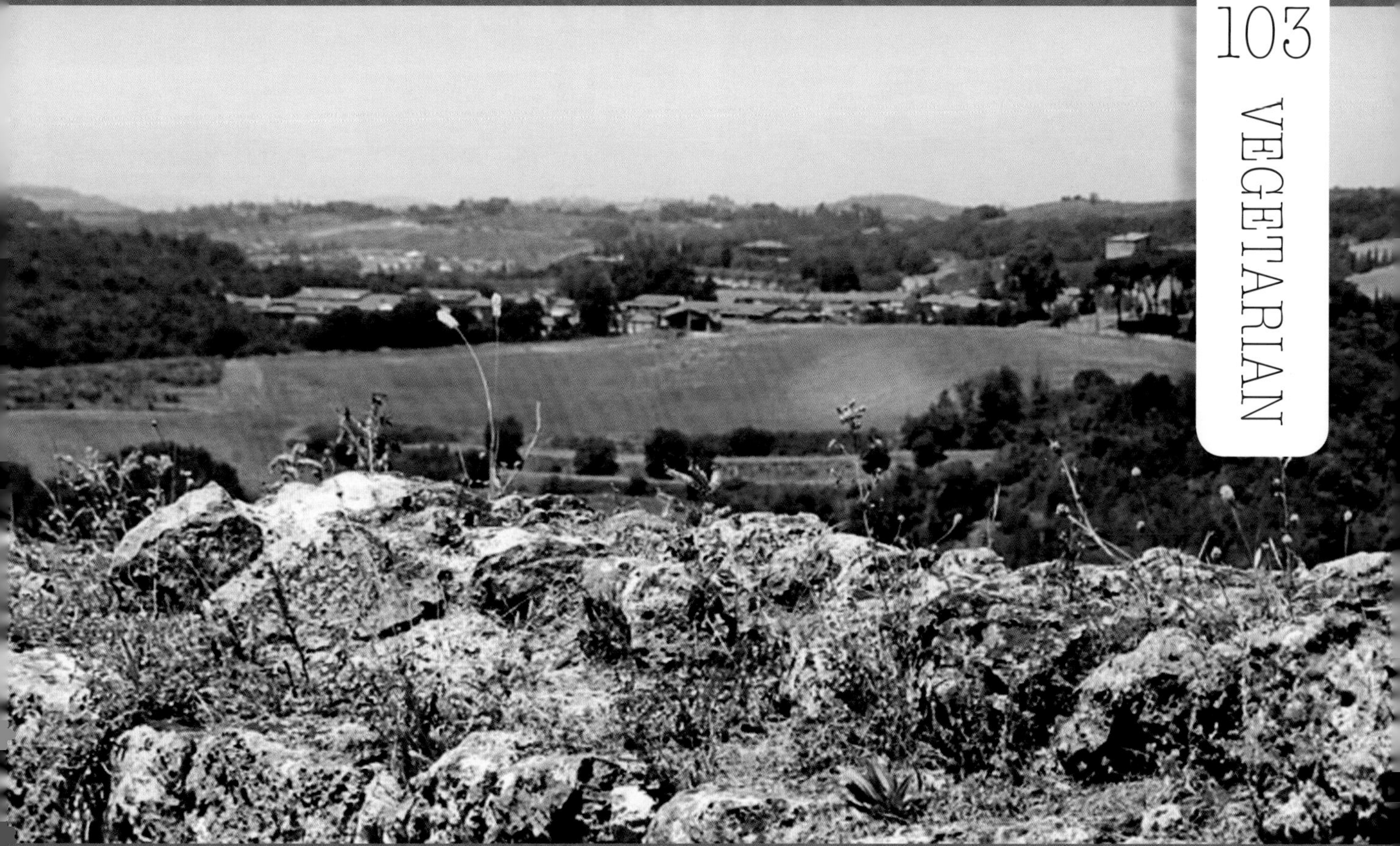

POST CARD

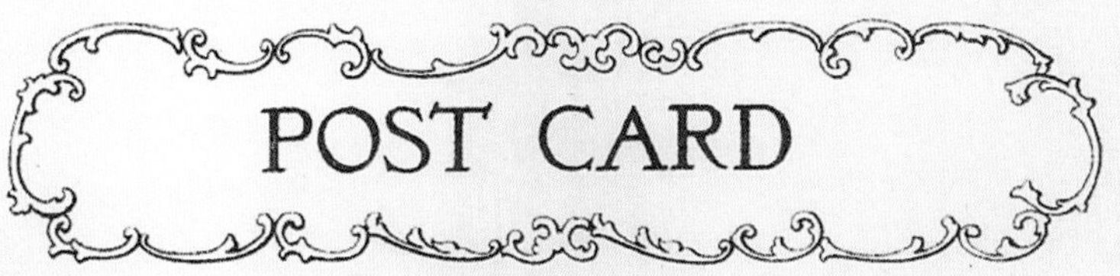

Place Stamp Here
Domestic One cent
Foreign Twocents

THIS SPACE MAY BE USED FOR WRITING.

San Gimiginano, Italy

THIS SIDE FOR THE ADDRESS ONLY.

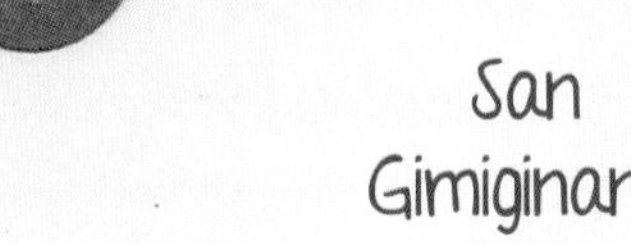

Stopping to rest while exploring, and noticed this beautiful pastoral view! Couldn't resist the photo opportunity!

Pushkar, India

chana masala

(Curried Chickpeas)

yield: 6 servings

ingredients

- 1 tbsp. olive oil
- 2 large white onions, diced
- 1 tbsp. minced garlic
- 1 tbsp. peeled, minced fresh ginger
- 1 tsp. garam masala
- 1 tsp. chili powder (optional)
- 1 tsp. salt or more if desired
- 4 large tomatoes, chopped
- 2 (15 oz.) cans chickpeas, rinsed and drained
- 1 bunch of fresh cilantro or parsley, chopped (optional)

directions

1. Heat oil in a large saucepan over medium-high heat.
2. Sauté onion, garlic, and ginger for 3-5 minutes.
3. Add spices and tomatoes and cook until soft, about 5-6 minutes, stirring occasionally.
4. Bring sauce to a boil, add chickpeas, and simmer for 20 minutes.
5. Garnish with cilantro or parsley if desired.

coconut da'al

(Lentil Stew)

yield: 4-6 servings

ingredients

- 3 cups water
- 1 cup dried red lentils
- 1 tsp. turmeric
- 1 tsp. cumin seeds
- 1 tbsp. coriander seeds
- ½ tsp. red chili flakes
- 1 (15 oz.) can light, unsweetened coconut milk
- 1 garlic clove, minced
- 1 tbsp. peeled, minced fresh ginger
- 3 large tomatoes, diced
- 2 cups fresh spinach
- ¼ tsp. ground cardamom
- ¼ tsp. ground cinnamon
- 1 tbsp. lemon juice
- salt and freshly ground black pepper to taste
- ¼ cup chopped fresh cilantro

directions

1. In a medium pot, bring water, lentils, and turmeric to a boil.
2. Cover the pot partially and simmer until soft, about 20 minutes, then drain.
3. In a separate pot, add cumin seeds, coriander seeds, and chili flakes. Toast over medium heat until seeds are fragrant and toasted, about 2-4 minutes.
4. Remove from heat. Add drained lentils, coconut milk, garlic, ginger, tomatoes, spinach, cardamom, cinnamon, and lemon juice and simmer, stirring occasionally for 10 minutes. Season with salt and pepper. Toss in cilantro and serve with Indian Spiced Roasted Chickpeas (recipe on pg. 68) if desired.

Pushkar, India – Cooking with Raj

After a long camel ride in the Rajasthani desert we finally break for lunch. If you're thinking of peanut butter and jelly sandwiches you are greatly mistaken. We retreated to a homemade meal cooked right on the spot by tour guide, Raj who showed us that shoes are not required when making salad with a hatchet.

eggplant parmigiana

yeild: 3-4 servings

ingredients

- 2 large eggs, plus more if needed
- 1 cup gluten free panko or bread crumbs
- salt and freshly ground black pepper to taste
- 1 large eggplant, cut into ½-inch thick rounds
- extra-virgin olive oil for frying
- 2 cups tomato sauce
- 2 cups shredded mozzarella cheese

directions

1. Preheat oven to 350°.
2. Crack and beat eggs in a bowl. In a second bowl, stir together panko or bread crumbs, salt, and pepper.
3. Dip eggplant slices first in egg then in panko or bread crumbs.
4. Heat oil in a large skillet over medium-high heat. Fry each slice until soft, about 2 minutes on each side.
5. In a 9x13 pan, create layers with eggplant and tomato sauce.
6. Top with mozzarella cheese.
7. Bake uncovered until cheese is melted, about 20 minutes.

Vernazza, Italy
One of my favorite spots in the world (as of yet). Introducing the whimsical village of Vernazza, Italy. This is my happy place.

Cinque Terre, Italy

I stopped to catch my breath and take this photo thinking I might die. Not from the incredible steepness of the mountain, but from the shame of being passed by 90 year-old women taking their daily morning hike.

eggplant risotto

yeild: 2 servings

ingredients

- 1 medium eggplant, halved
- 2 tbsp. olive oil
- 2 ¼ cups water
- 1 cup uncooked brown rice
- ¼ cup dry white wine
- ¼ cup lemon juice
- 1 tbsp. butter
- ½ cup chopped fresh parsley, plus more for garnish if desired
- ½ cup chopped fresh dill, plus more for garnish if desired
- ½ cup chopped fresh basil, plus more for garnish if desired

directions

1. Preheat oven to 400°.
2. Rub eggplant with oil then bake on a baking sheet for 1 hour, turning once halfway through baking time.
3. Pour water into a medium sauce pan, add rice, cover, and bring to a boil then reduce heat to low and let simmer until water is absorbed, about 30 minutes.
4. When rice is fully cooked, add wine, lemon juice, butter, and herbs and cook over low heat until rice is soft and creamy.
5. Remove from heat. Scoop out roasted eggplant from the skin and mix the flesh in with the rice.
6. Serve warm and garnish with additional herbs if desired.

garlic & basil spaghetti squash

yield: 4 servings

ingredients

- 5 tbsp. olive oil
- 1 large white onion, sliced into rings
- 2-3 garlic cloves, chopped
- 2 cups cooked, shredded spaghetti squash, (noted below)
- 1 cup grape tomatoes, halved
- ½ cup basil leaves or more if desired
- salt and freshly ground black pepper to taste
- 1 cup diced buffalo mozzarella (optional)

directions

1. Heat oil in a large pan over medium-high heat. Sauté onion and garlic until onion is translucent and garlic is golden brown, about 5 minutes.
2. Add spaghetti squash, tomatoes, basil, salt, and pepper.
3. Mix for 2 minutes then serve warm and top with mozzarella if desired.

how to cook a spaghetti squash:

1. Score the whole squash with a knife 8-10 times to help vent out steam. This will prevent your squash from exploding within the microwave.
2. Place the squash on a microwave safe dish and add a little water to the bottom, to help from having the squash dry out.
3. Microwave your squash in 5 minute increments until fork tender. Depending on the strength of your microwave, this could take anywhere from 5-25 minutes.
4. Once cooked, allow to cool for 10 minutes. Then, cut in half lengthwise and using a spoon, scoop out the seeds and discard.
5. Using a fork, scrape the flesh against the grain to create your spaghetti squash "noodle" strands.

Burano, Italy
When you pass a blue house with a blue boat under a clear blue sky, you know you are in the Crayola crayon colored village of Burano.

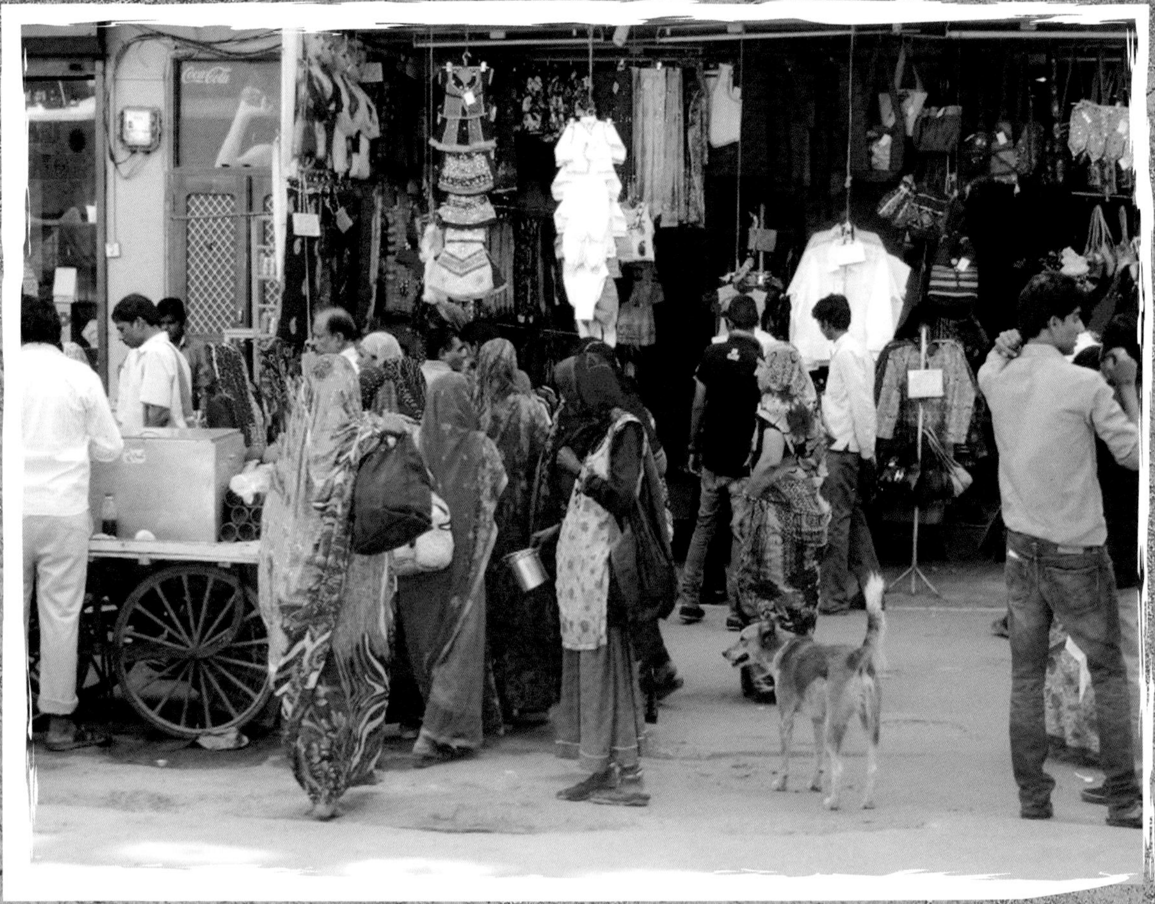

POST CARD

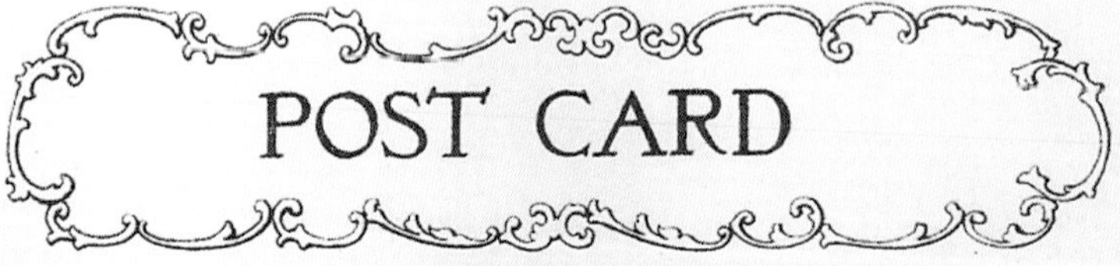

Place Stamp Here
Domestic One cent
Foreign Twocents

THIS SPACE MAY BE USED FOR WRITING.

Pushkar,
India

THIS SIDE FOR THE ADDRESS ONLY.

Breathtaking colors here on the street in Pushkar, India. Take a lesson New York: Fuchsia is the new black!!

malai kofta

(Potato & Veggie Balls)

yield: 3-4 servings

ingredients

- 4 cups water
- 4 medium all-purpose potatoes, peeled and diced
- 1 cup mixed vegetables (carrots, peas, and sweet corn kernels)
- 1 cup paneer, farmer cheese, or sour cream
- 2 tbsp. heavy cream
- 1 tsp. ground cumin
- 1 tsp. ground coriander
- ½ tsp. chili powder or more if desired (optional)
- salt to taste
- 1 cup extra-virgin olive oil for frying

Sauce:

- 3 tbsp. extra-virgin olive oil
- 2 large white onions, diced
- 2 tbsp. tomato paste
- 1 tbsp. peeled, chopped fresh ginger
- 1 tbsp. chopped garlic
- 2 tbsp. ground coriander
- 2 tbsp. garam masala
- 1 tbsp. ground cumin
- ½ tsp. chili powder or more if desired (optional)
- cooked brown rice (optional)

directions

1. Pour water into a large pot, then add potatoes and mixed vegetables. Cover and simmer until potatoes can be pierced easily with a fork, about 6-8 minutes. Remove from heat and strain.
2. Mash three of the potatoes, mixed vegetables, paneer, farmer cheese, or sour cream, and heavy cream together. Add Kofta spices and mix well. The resulting dough should be firm. If not, add as much of the fourth boiled potato as needed. Season with salt.
3. Roll dough into "meatball" sized rounds. Heat oil for frying over medium heat and fry rounds, turning them occasionally in the pan, until golden. Drain on paper towels and set aside.
4. For the sauce, heat oil in a deep pan over medium-high heat and sauté onions until translucent, about 5 minutes. Put cooked onions, tomato paste, ginger, garlic, coriander, garam masala, cumin, and chili powder, if using, in a blender and blend until smooth. Remove from blender and put back into pan. Fry until oil begins to separate.
5. Bring sauce to a boil, then reduce to a simmer. Gently add koftas to sauce and cook uncovered for 2-3 minutes. Turn off heat, cover, and allow to sit for 5 minutes. Serve hot with brown rice if desired.

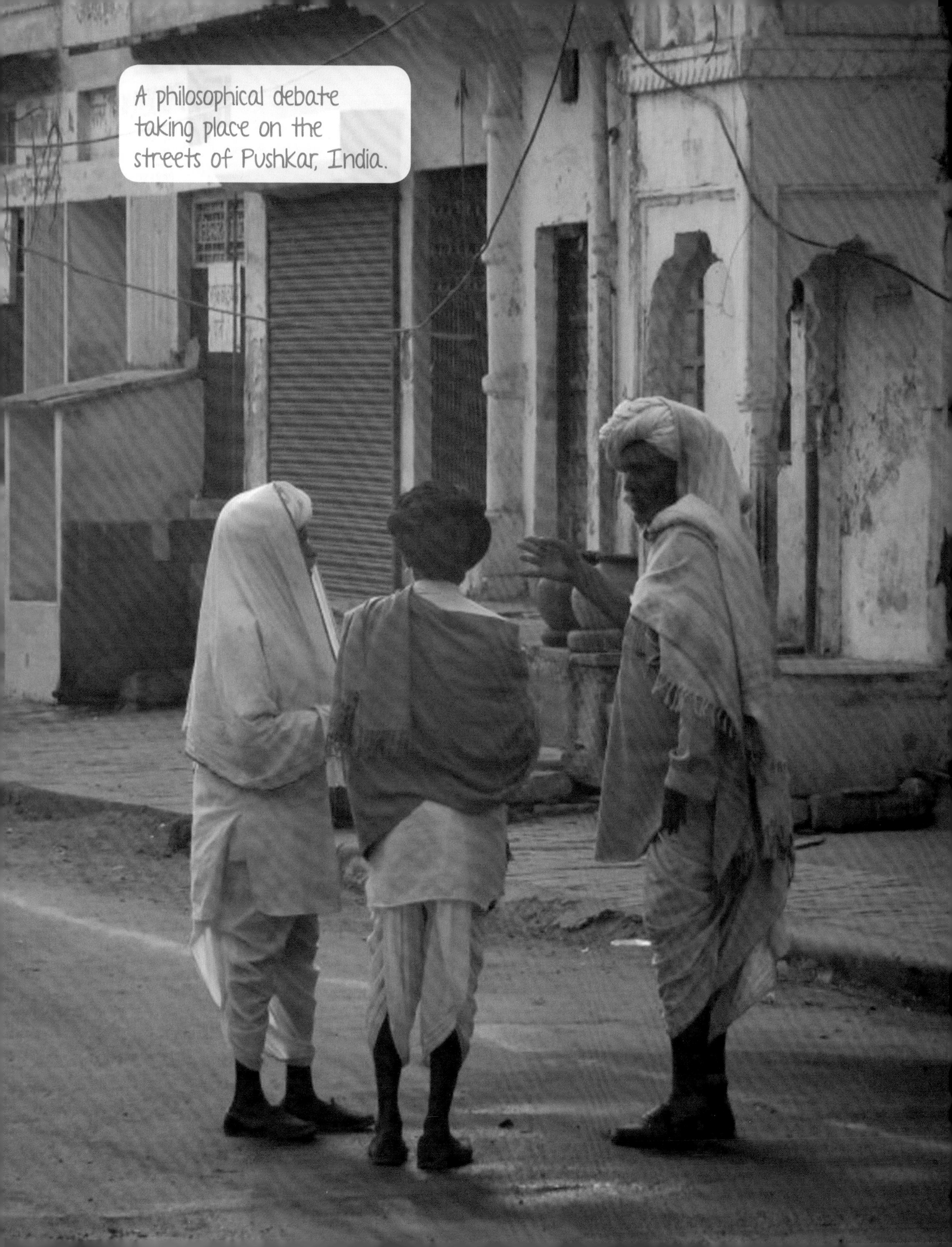

A philosophical debate taking place on the streets of Pushkar, India.

palak paneer

(Curried Spinach, Tomato & Cheese Purée)

yield: 2 servings

ingredients

- 2 tbsp. extra-virgin olive oil or unsalted butter
- ½ -¾ tsp. cumin seeds
- 1 medium yellow onion, finely chopped
- 2 tbsp. chopped garlic
- 1-2 Thai green chilies, deseeded, stemmed, and chopped
- 1 tsp. peeled, chopped fresh ginger
- 1 medium tomato, chopped
- ½ tsp. chili powder
- ¼ tsp. turmeric
- 2 cups chopped fresh spinach
- a pinch of salt
- ½ tsp. garam masala
- ½ cup paneer, farmer cheese, or sour cream
- 1 tsp. crushed fennel leaves (optional)
- cooked rice and sour cream (optional)

directions

1. Heat oil or butter in a pot over medium-high heat.
2. Add cumin seeds and allow to sputter, then add onion and cook until translucent, about 5 minutes. Add garlic, chilies, ginger, and tomato and cook until soft, then add chili powder and turmeric. Cook for a few seconds while stirring then add spinach. Simmer until spinach is cooked, about 6-7 minutes.
3. Add salt and garam masala. Stir, then add paneer, farmer cheese, or sour cream, cooking sauce until it becomes smooth and creamy. Stir in crushed fenugreek leaves, if using.
4. Turn off heat. Using an immersion blender, purée until almost smooth. Serve with rice and sour cream for topping if desired.

pasta with spinach & arugula pesto

yield: 3-4 servings

ingredients

Pesto:

- 1 garlic clove
- 2 cups fresh spinach
- ½ cup fresh basil
- 3-4 ½ cups fresh arugula leaves, divided
- ¾ cup grated Parmesan cheese
- 3 tbsp. olive oil
- salt and freshly ground black pepper to taste
- ½ lb. gluten free pasta, cooked (I prefer Lundberg Farms gluten free brown rice Rotini pasta)
- 1 cup cherry tomatoes, halved
- 3-4 cups fresh arugula

directions

1. Prepare pasta according to the directions on the package.
2. In a food processor, roughly chop the garlic clove.
3. To create the pesto, add spinach, basil, ½ cup arugula, Parmesan cheese, and oil, and process until smooth, about 1 minute. Season with salt and pepper.
4. Add pesto to cooked cooked pasta, toss with cherry tomatoes, and serve on a bed of the remaining 3-4 cups arugula.

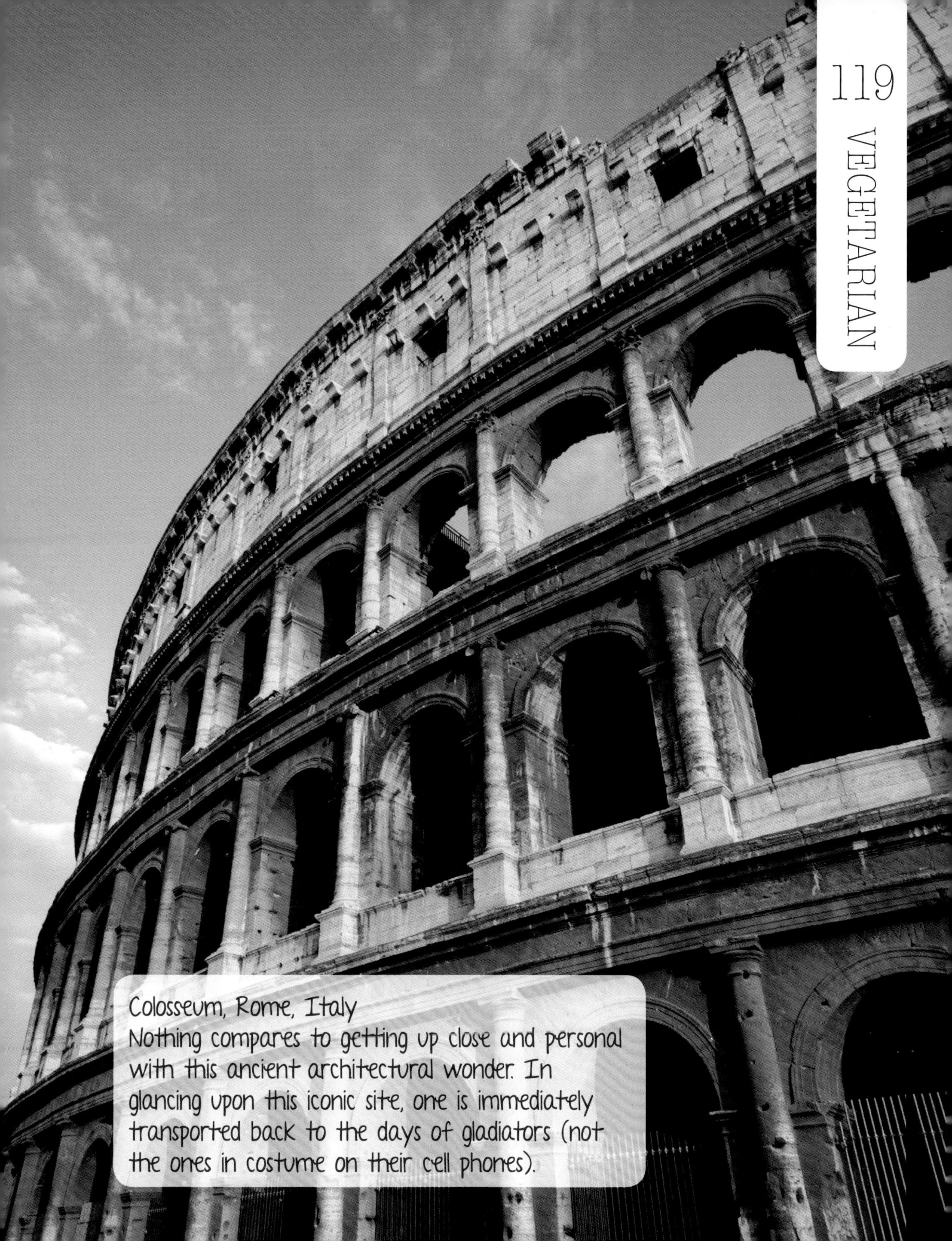

Colosseum, Rome, Italy
Nothing compares to getting up close and personal with this ancient architectural wonder. In glancing upon this iconic site, one is immediately transported back to the days of gladiators (not the ones in costume on their cell phones).

quinoa veggie biryani

(Indian Spiced Quinoa with Veggies)

yield: 2-4 servings

ingredients

Quinoa:
- 1 tbsp. unsalted butter or olive oil
- 2 tbsp. blanched, sliced almonds
- 1 tsp. cumin seeds
- ½ tsp. turmeric
- ½ tsp. ground cardamom
- ½ tsp. ground cinnamon
- ¼ tsp. coriander seeds
- ¾ cup uncooked quinoa, rinsed
- 1 ½ cups water
- 1 tsp. salt

Vegetables:
- 2 tbsp. unsalted butter or olive oil
- 1 small yellow onion, thinly sliced
- 2 garlic cloves, minced
- 1 tbsp. peeled, minced fresh ginger
- 2 tbsp. blanched sliced almonds, plus more for garnish
- 1 tsp. cumin seeds
- 1 tsp. ground cardamom
- ½ tsp. ground coriander
- 5 cups small cauliflower florets
- ½ cup cut up green beans
- 3 small new potatoes, peeled and cubed
- 1 carrot, cut into 1-inch pieces
- 1 tsp. salt
- ¾ cup water

directions

1. To make the quinoa, melt butter or oil in a medium saucepan over medium heat. Add almonds, cumin seeds, turmeric, cardamom, cinnamon, and coriander seeds and cook, stirring, until seeds are toasted and fragrant, about 2 minutes. Add uncooked quinoa and cook, stirring until toasted, about 1 minute more. Add water and salt and bring to a boil.
2. Once boiling, reduce heat to a simmer. Cover and cook until quinoa is tender, about 15 minutes.
3. Remove from heat and let sit, covered, for 10 minutes.
4. To make the vegetables, melt butter or oil in a large pot. Add onion and cook over medium-high heat, stirring often, until translucent, about 5 minutes. Add garlic and ginger stirring until fragrant then add almonds, cumin seeds, cardamom, and coriander and stir until toasted and fragrant. Stir in cauliflower, green beans, potatoes, carrot, and salt.
5. Raise heat to high, pour in water, cover, and cook for about 10 minutes, stirring occasionally.
6. Combine quinoa and vegetable mixtures. Top with additional almonds and serve hot.

My host and I outside his houseboat on Dal Lake in Kashmir, India

Cotopaxi, Ecuador

rainbow quesadilla pizza

yield: 4 servings

ingredients

- 1 large red onion, diced
- 1 jalapeño pepper, deseeded, stemmed, and diced
- 1 garlic clove, sliced
- 3 tbsp. olive oil
- 1 red bell pepper, deseeded, stemmed, and diced
- 1 orange bell pepper, deseeded, stemmed, and diced
- 1 yellow bell pepper, deseeded, stemmed, and diced
- 1 tsp. chopped fresh oregano or ¼ tsp. dried oregano
- ¼ tsp. salt
- 4 (8-inch) corn tortillas
- 4 cups shredded fresh mozzarella cheese
- 1 tbsp. chopped fresh cilantro
- salsa verde and sour cream (optional)

directions

1. Preheat oven to 400°.
2. For filling, in a large skillet, cook onion, jalapeño, and garlic in hot oil over medium-high heat until onion is translucent and garlic is golden brown, about 5 minutes. Stir in bell peppers, oregano, and salt and heat through until peppers are soft, about 2 minutes.
3. Place tortillas on a baking sheet and top with shredded cheese, then place filling on top of cheese or vice versa according to preference. Bake for 10-15 minutes depending on desired doneness, 10 minutes for melted cheese or 15 minutes for cheese that is golden brown. Garnish with cilantro and serve with salsa verde and sour cream if desired.

Montmartre, France

sage & onion spaghetti squash soufflé

yield: 6 servings

ingredients

- ½ cup butter
- 2 large white onions, diced
- salt and freshly ground black pepper to taste
- 2 cups cooked, shredded spaghetti squash (noted below)
- 3 tbsp. chopped fresh sage
- 3 large eggs
- 6 garlic cloves, chopped

directions

1. Preheat oven to 400˚ and grease a 9-inch pie dish.
2. In a very large skillet, melt butter over low heat. Add onions and a generous pinch of salt and pepper and cook, stirring occasionally, until onions are soft and golden, about 30 minutes. Let onions cool completely.
3. In a bowl, mix together spaghetti squash, cooked onions, sage, eggs, garlic, salt, and pepper and pour into the prepared pie dish. Bake until crust is golden and crispy, about 45 minutes. If soufflé is watery, carefully pour off excess liquid and bake off some of the moisture for about 5-10 minutes.

how to cook a spaghetti squash:

1. Score the whole squash with a knife 8-10 times to help vent out steam. This will prevent your squash from exploding within the microwave.
2. Place the squash on a microwave safe dish and add a little water to the bottom, to help from having the squash dry out.
3. Microwave your squash in 5 minute increments until it is fork tender. Depending on the strength of your microwave, this could take anywhere from 5-25 minutes.
4. Once cooked, allow to cool for 10 minutes. Then, cut in half lengthwise and using a spoon, scoop out the seeds and discard.
5. Using a fork, scrape the flesh against the grain to create your spaghetti squash "noodle" strands.

tofu in black bean sauce

yield: 3-4 servings

ingredients

- 1 lb. block extra-firm tofu
- 4 garlic cloves, chopped
- 1 ½-inches fresh ginger, peeled and chopped
- 2 tbsp. Chinese fermented black beans, rinsed and drained
- 1 ½ cups water
- 4 tbsp. gluten free soy sauce
- 1 tbsp. granulated sugar or agave nectar
- 2 tsp. cider vinegar
- 2 tbsp. cornstarch, dissolved in 4 tbsp. cold water
- ¼ cup extra-virgin olive oil, divided
- cooked brown rice and broccoli (optional)

directions

1. Remove tofu from packaging liquid. Place tofu in a strainer over a bowl and place a weight on top to drain excess liquid.
2. To create the sauce, place garlic and ginger in a food processor or blender and grind. Stop the machine, add beans, and pulse until coarsely chopped. Set aside in a bowl.
3. In a separate bowl, stir together water, soy sauce, sugar or agave nectar, vinegar, and dissolved cornstarch.
4. Heat 2 tbsp. oil in a saucepan over medium-high heat. Stir-fry garlic, ginger, and bean mixture until fragrant. Stir liquid mixture and add it to the pan. Bring sauce to a boil, stirring occasionally, then remove pan from heat and set aside.
5. Remove weight from tofu block and cut tofu into cubes. Heat the remaining 2 tbsp. oil in a medium frying pan until sizzling. Blot up any excess moisture on the tofu with a paper towel before placing it in the skillet. Fry tofu cubes on all sides, turning only when undersides are golden and crisp, about 3-4 minutes on each side. Give tofu one last flip on a paper towel to sop up any excess oil, then add it to the sauce. Serve with brown rice and broccoli if desired.

Pushkar, India
1-800-Schleppers.

vegetable dhansak

(Hearty Veggie & Lentil Stew)

yield: 6-8 servings

ingredients

- 5 cups water
- 1 ½ cups assorted lentils
- 4-5 medium tomatoes, chopped
- 2 medium all-purpose potatoes, peeled and chopped
- 2 medium eggplants, chopped
- 1 small pumpkin or butternut squash, peeled, deseeded, and chopped

Garlic-Chili Paste:

- 12 garlic cloves, minced
- 1 tbsp. peeled, minced fresh ginger
- 1 tbsp. coriander seeds
- 1 ½ tsp. cumin seeds
- ½ tsp. ground cinnamon
- ¼ tsp. whole cloves
- 1-2 red chilies, deseeded and stemmed or ½ tbsp. chili powder
- 2 Thai green chilies, deseeded and stemmed
- ¼ cup water
- 3-4 tsp. tamarind pulp
- 4-5 tbsp. butter
- 1 large white onion, chopped
- 1 tsp. fennel seeds

directions

1. Set 5 cups water to boil in a large Dutch oven or pot. Rinse lentils and add to boiling water along with tomatoes, potatoes, eggplants, and pumpkin or squash. Cover and cook until tender, about 15 minutes.
2. Meanwhile, prepare the Garlic-Chili Paste by grinding garlic, ginger, coriander seeds, cumin seeds, cinnamon, cloves, chilies or chili powder, and ¼ cup water together. Add tamarind pulp and set aside.
3. Melt butter in a large sauté pan, then add onion and fennel seeds and sauté over medium-high heat until onion is translucent, about 5 minutes. Add Garlic-Chili Paste and sauté for 3-4 minutes.
4. Combine onion mixture and lentil mixture and let simmer for 10 minutes.

vegetable jalfrezi

(Spicy Veggie & Cheese Stew)

yield: 4 servings

ingredients

- 1 tbsp. olive oil
- 1 tsp. cumin seeds
- 2 medium yellow onions, sliced
- 2 red bell peppers, deseeded, stemmed, and chopped
- 2 medium tomatoes, chopped
- 1 carrot, diced
- 1 ½ cups chopped green beans
- 1 cup cut up cauliflower
- ½ cup green peas
- 2-3 green chili peppers, deseeded, stemmed, and diced
- 2 tbsp. peeled, minced fresh ginger
- 2 tsp. dried fennel leaves (optional)
- 1 tsp. chili powder (optional)
- 1 tsp. garam masala
- ½ tsp. turmeric
- 1 ½ tsp. salt
- 1 cup paneer, farmer cheese, or sour cream

directions

1. Heat oil in a pot over medium-high heat. Add cumin seeds and allow to sputter.
2. Add onion and sauté over medium-high heat until translucent, about 5 minutes, then add all vegetables and spices and mix well. Cover and cook until soft, about 20-25 minutes.
3. When vegetables are soft, stir in paneer, farmer cheese, or sour cream and cook, covered, over low heat, for 5 minutes. Serve hot.

Kashmir, India
Vibrant reflections of a colorful houseboat on Dal Lake.

Fish

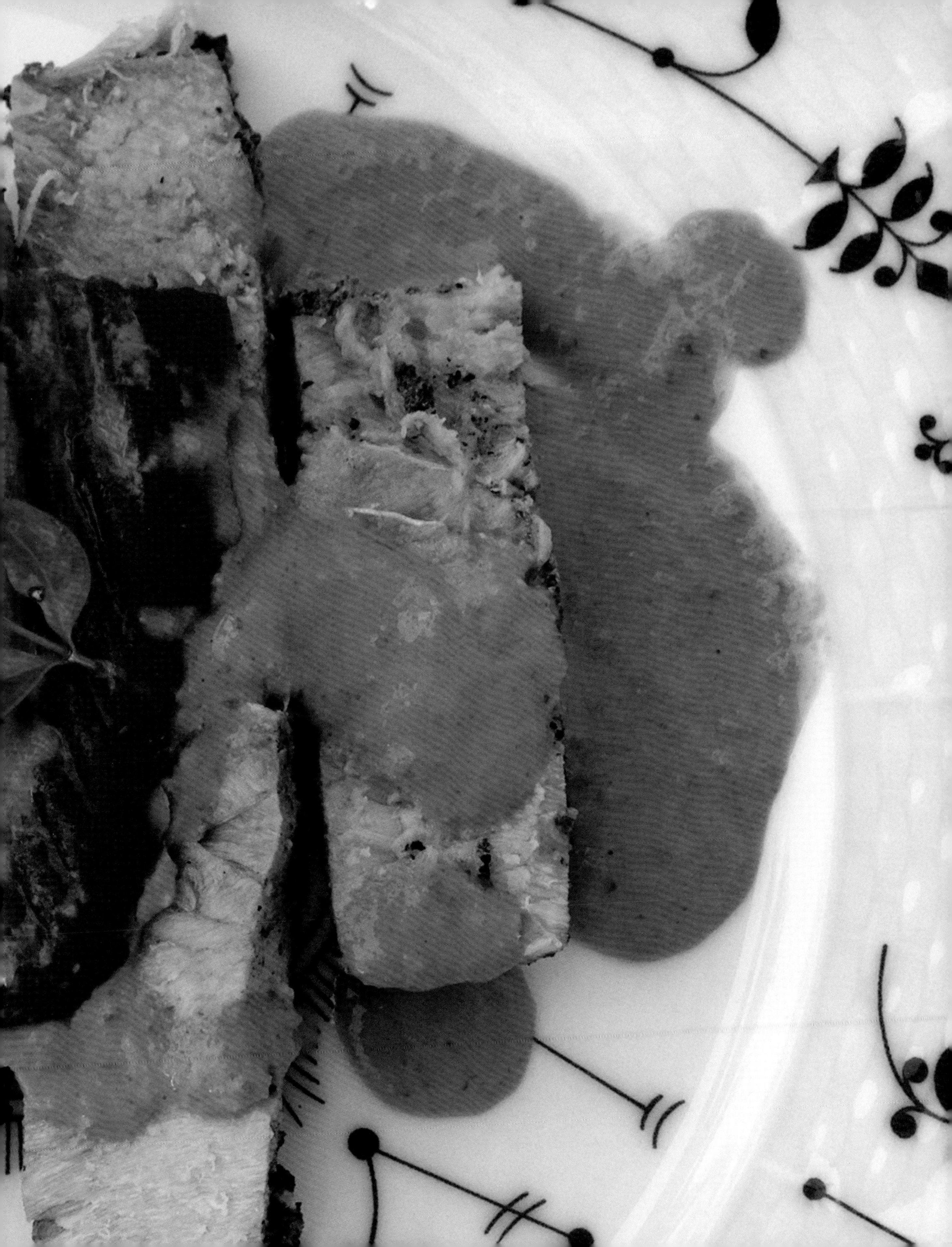

fish tacos with creamed corn

yield: 6 servings

ingredients

- 2 lbs. fresh or frozen cod, or red snapper, cut into bite-sized pieces
- salt and freshly ground black pepper to taste
- 4 tbsp. lemon juice
- 4 cups finely shredded cabbage
- ½ cup chopped scallions
- ½ cup chopped fresh cilantro or parsley
- 3 tbsp. white vinegar
- 2 tbsp. light extra-virgin olive or canola oil
- 1 tsp. granulated sugar or agave nectar
- salt to taste
- 1 large egg, lightly beaten
- 1 ½ cups gluten free panko or bread crumbs
- ¼ cup extra-virgin olive oil for frying
- 12 (6-inch) corn tortillas, warmed
- 2 avocados, sliced
- lime wedges (optional)

directions

1. Rinse fish and pat dry with paper towels. Sprinkle fish with salt, pepper, and lemon juice and set aside.
2. In a medium bowl, combine cabbage, scallions, cilantro or parsley, vinegar, oil, sugar or agave nectar, and salt. Toss well to combine, then cover and chill until ready to serve.
3. Place egg and panko or bread crumbs in separate bowls. Coat fish first in egg, shaking off excess, then with panko or bread crumbs.
4. In a large skillet, heat oil over medium heat and fry fish in hot oil for 2-4 minutes or until crispy and golden, turning once halfway through frying time. Drain on paper towels.
5. To serve, place one or two fish pieces in the center of each warm tortilla. Top with chilled cabbage mixture, avocado slices, and creamed corn. Serve with lime wedges if desired.

creamed corn topping

yield: 6 servings

ingredients

Creamed Corn Topping:

- 1 tbsp. butter
- 1 small red onion, finely chopped
- 8-10 oz. fresh or frozen corn
- ¾ cup water
- ½ cup heavy cream
- 1 tsp. granulated sugar or agave nectar
- salt and freshly ground black pepper to taste

directions

1. In a medium saucepan, melt butter over medium-high heat. Add onion and cook, stirring occasionally, until translucent, about 5 minutes. Add corn kernels and water. Bring to a boil, then reduce to a simmer. Cover and cook until corn is tender, about 10-15 minutes.
2. Add cream and sugar or agave nectar. Continue simmering, until cream has thickened, about 4-6 minutes. Season with salt and pepper.

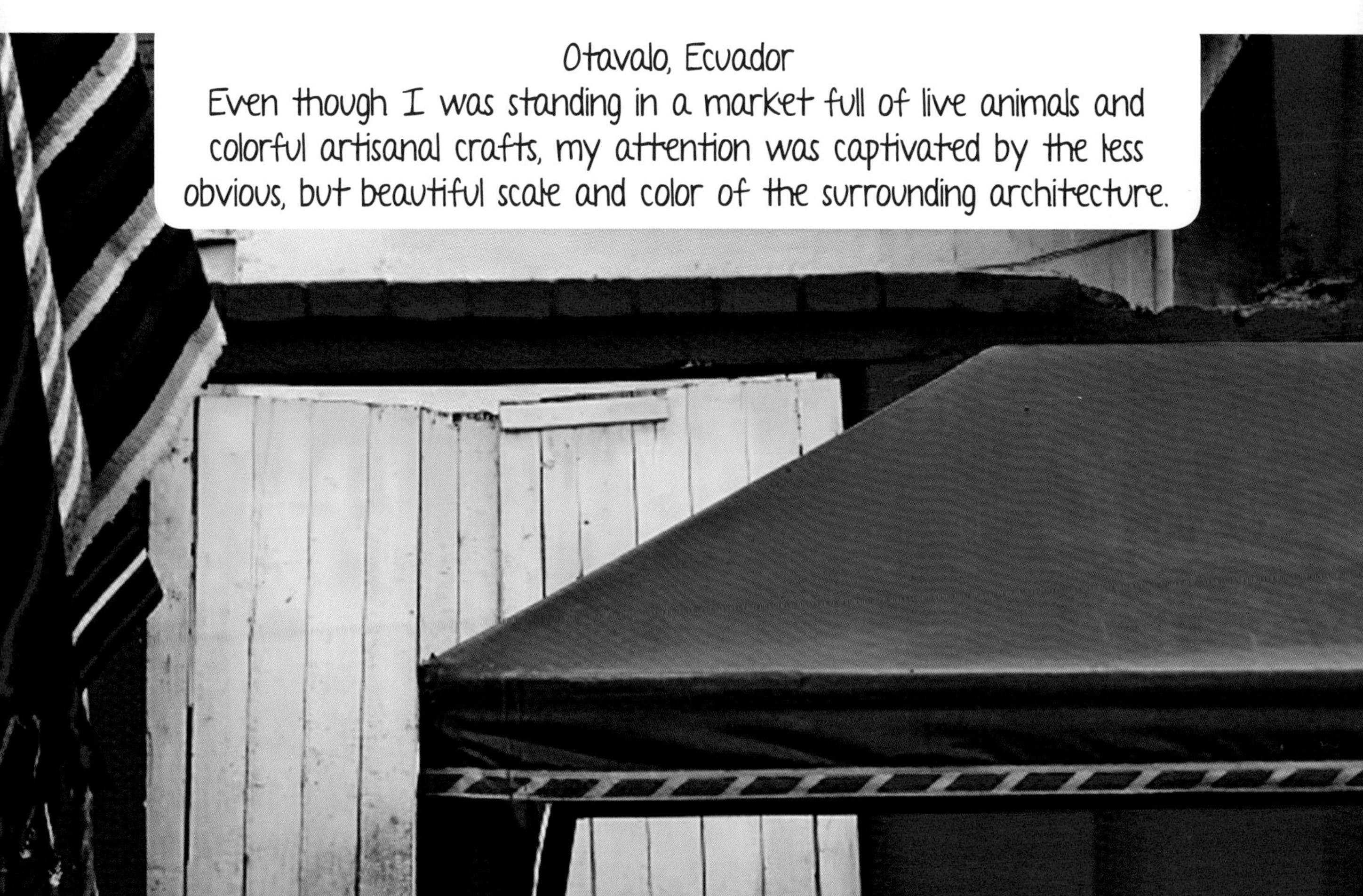

Otavalo, Ecuador

Even though I was standing in a market full of live animals and colorful artisanal crafts, my attention was captivated by the less obvious, but beautiful scale and color of the surrounding architecture.

Place Stamp Here
Domestic One cent
Foreign Twocents

THIS SPACE MAY BE USED FOR WRITING.

Venice,
Italy

THIS SIDE FOR THE ADDRESS ONLY.

A classic Venetian scene, gondolas and all, greets one right outside the renowned San Marco Basilica.

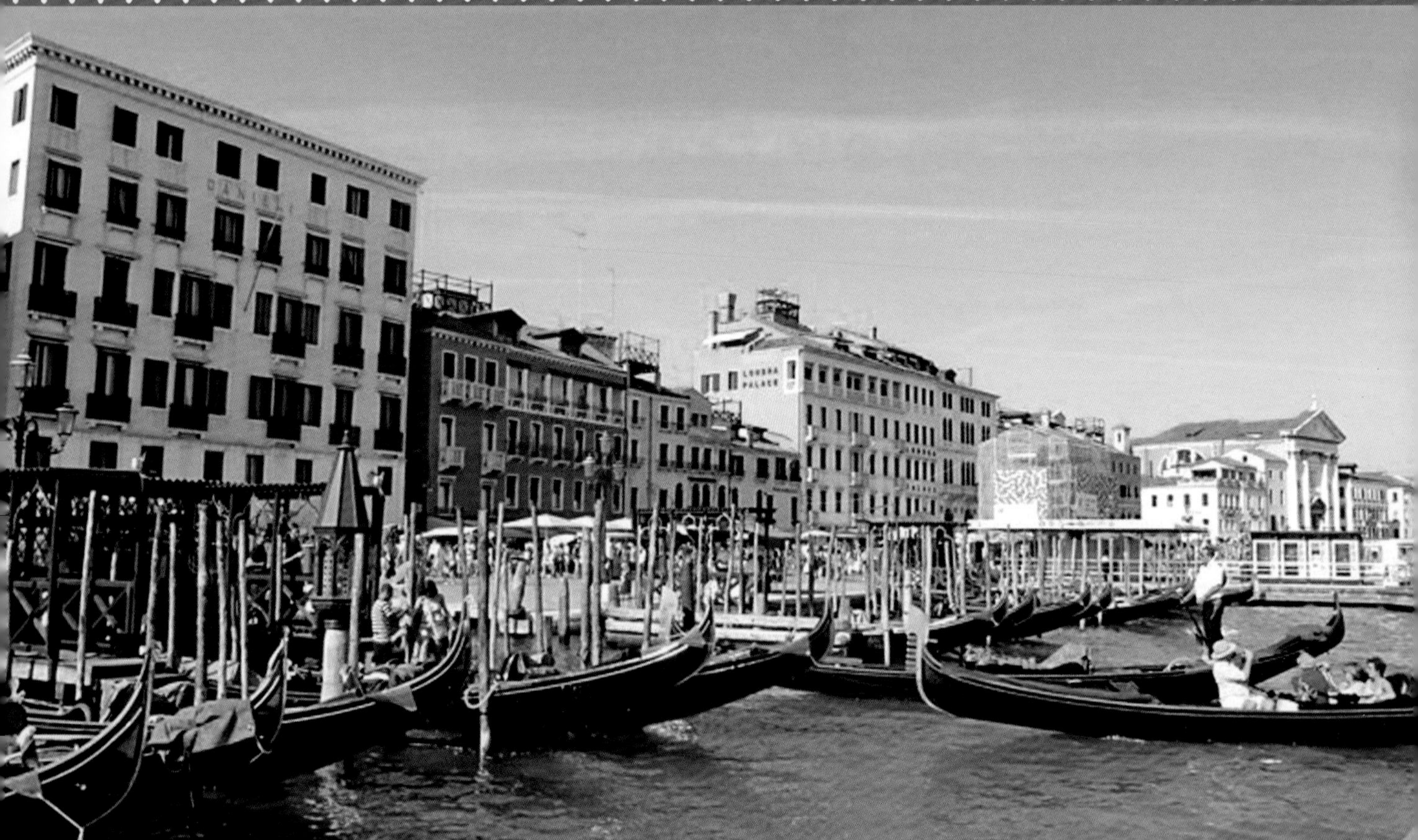

halibut al spinachi

yield: 4 servings

ingredients

- 4 (4 oz.) halibut fillets
- ¼ tsp. salt
- ¼ tsp. freshly ground black pepper
- ½ stick or ¼ cup butter
- 3 tbsp. extra-virgin olive oil
- zest of ½ lemon
- juice of 1 lemon or 3 tbsp. lemon juice
- 2 tbsp. capers in juice
- 1 garlic clove, chopped
- 2 tbsp. chopped fresh parsley

directions

1. Preheat oven to 375°.
2. Season halibut with salt and pepper.
3. Melt butter and olive oil in a medium sized skillet over medium heat. Add lemon zest, lemon juice, capers, and garlic. Bring to a simmer. Add halibut to pan and sauté until brown, about 2 minutes on each side.
4. Remove skillet from stove top and place directly in oven until cooked through, about 6 minutes.
5. Carefully remove hot skillet from oven. Garnish with parsley and drizzle sauce over halibut. Serve immediately.

moroccan baked salmon with herb relish

yield: 6 servings

ingredients

Herb Relish:

- ¼ cup olive oil
- ¼ cup mayonnaise or plain yogurt
- 1 tbsp. lemon juice
- 3-4 peeled garlic cloves or more if desired
- 1 small red onion, chopped
- 1 cup fresh flat-leaf parsley, thick stems trimmed
- 2 tbsp. fresh oregano
- 2 tbsp. fresh dill
- ¼ tsp. red pepper flakes (optional)
- salt and freshly ground black pepper to taste

Salmon:

- 1 large white onion, diced
- 5 tbsp. olive oil
- ½ red bell pepper, deseeded, stemmed, and diced
- ½ yellow bell pepper, deseeded, stemmed, and diced
- ½ orange bell pepper, deseeded, stemmed, and diced
- ½ cup pitted green olives
- 6 (6 oz.) salmon fillets
- 2 tsp. ground cumin
- 1 tsp. turmeric
- salt and freshly ground black pepper to taste

directions

Herb Relish:

1. Place olive oil, mayonnaise or yogurt, lemon juice, garlic, red onion, parsley, oregano, dill, red pepper flakes, if using, salt, and pepper in a blender and blend until smooth. Refrigerate until chilled.

Fish:

1. Preheat oven to 350°.
2. Sauté onion in oil over medium-high heat, stirring occasionally, until translucent, about 5 minutes, then add peppers and olives and cook an additional 5 minutes or until peppers are soft.
3. Place salmon in a 9x13 pan and season with cumin, turmeric, salt, and pepper.
4. Pour sautéed onion, peppers, and olives on top of seasoned salmon.
5. Cover and bake until salmon is cooked through, about 30 minutes.
6. Serve salmon with chilled Herb Relish.

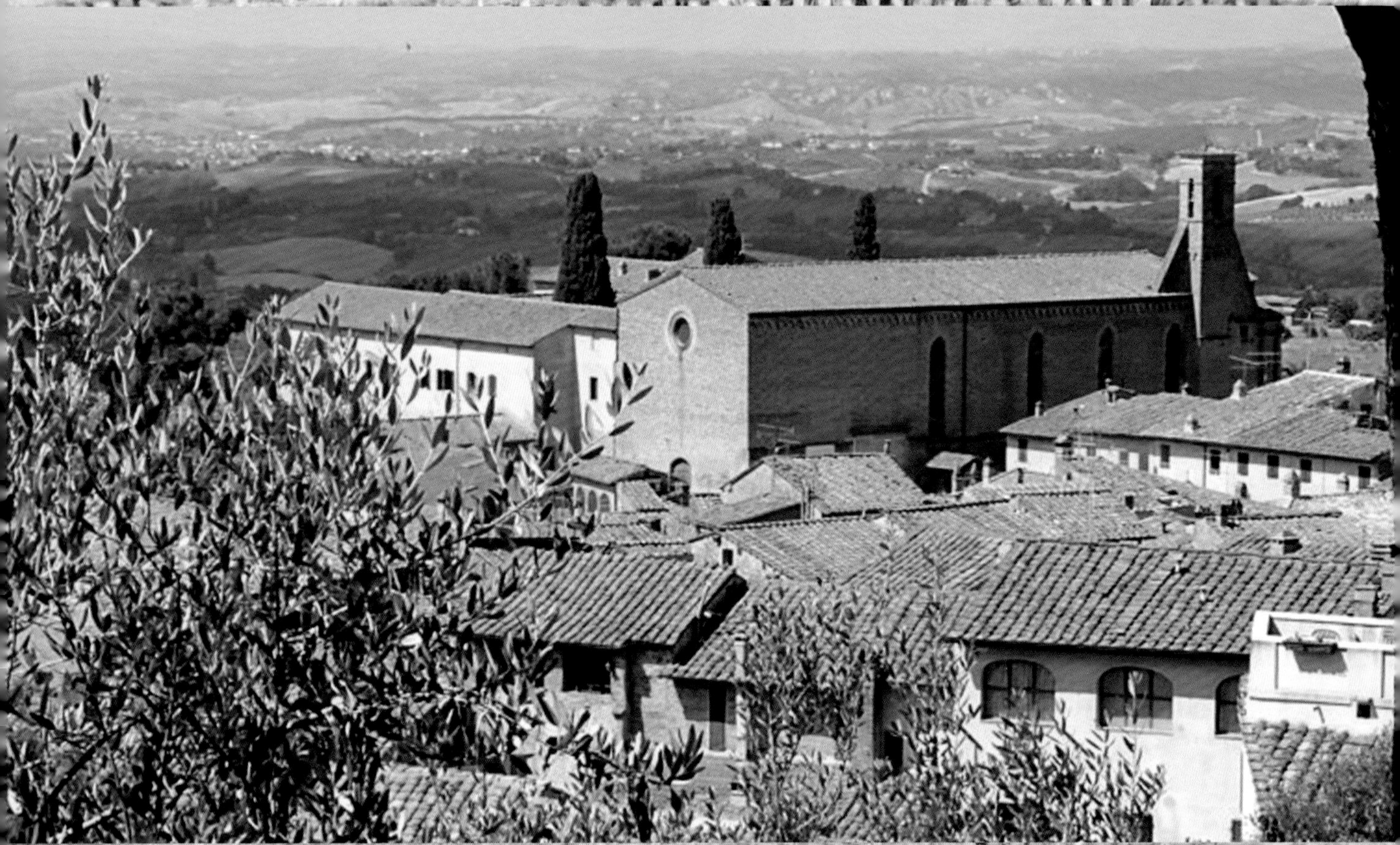

POST CARD

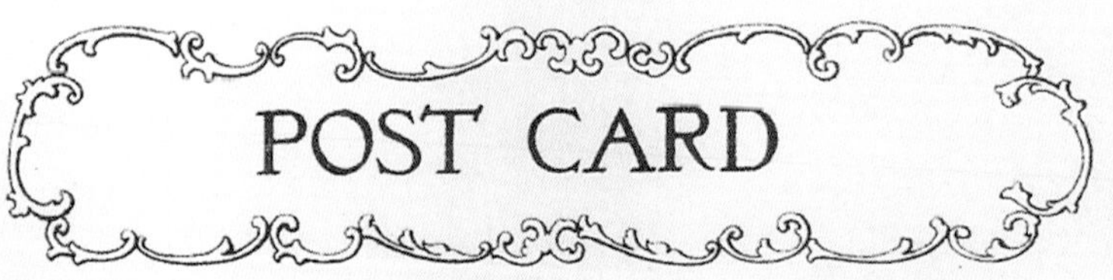

Place Stamp Here
Domestic
One cent
Foreign
Twocents

THIS SPACE MAY BE USED FOR WRITING.

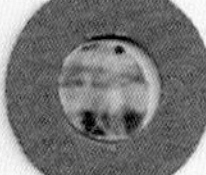

Tuscany,
Italy

THIS SIDE FOR THE ADDRESS ONLY.

Olive trees, cyprus trees
and terra cotta roofs ....
a classic Tuscan landscape.

olive tapenade roasted salmon

yield: 4 servings

ingredients

Tapenade:
- 1 cup pitted green olives
- 1 cup pitted black olives
- ½ cup mayonnaise or plain yogurt or ¼ cup olive oil
- salt and freshly ground black pepper to taste

Salmon:
- 4 (6 oz.) salmon fillets
- 2 tbsp. olive oil
- 4 tbsp. lemon juice
- salt and pepper to taste

directions

1. Preheat oven to 350°.
2. Place olives, mayonnaise or yogurt or oil, salt, and pepper in a blender and blend until mixture is smooth.
3. Place salmon on a baking sheet, brush with oil, sprinkle with lemon juice, then season with salt and pepper. Spoon tapenade over salmon to coat it completely.
4. Bake until salmon is cooked through, about 20 minutes.

Amazon Region, Ecuador
Living proof that pineapple doesn't grow in a can.

pineapple salmon skewers

yield: 6-8 servings

ingredients

- 4 tbsp. olive oil, plus more for coating skewers
- 3 tbsp. gluten free soy sauce
- 3 tbsp. sriracha hot sauce
- 2 tbsp. honey
- 2 tbsp. lime juice
- 2 garlic cloves, minced
- 1 (1 ½ lb.) salmon fillet, skin removed and cut into 1-inch pieces
- 1 large white onion, cut into large chunks
- 2 red bell peppers, deseeded, stemmed, and cut into large chunks
- 1 pineapple, pealed, cored, and cut into 1-inch chunks

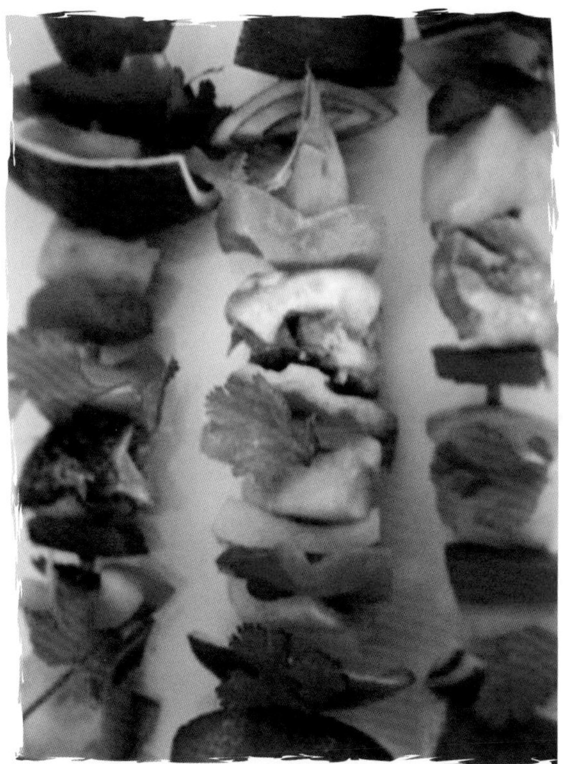

directions

1. In a medium bowl, whisk together oil, soy sauce, sriracha, honey, lime juice, and garlic.
2. Place salmon in the marinade mixture and stir gently to coat. Refrigerate for 1-2 hours.
3. Thread salmon, onion, red pepper, and pineapple chunks onto skewers. Be sure to apply a light coat of oil on the skewers prior to threading.
4. Preheat grill to medium-high heat, if using, or set oven to broil.
5. Cook skewers about 2 minutes on each side, watching closely to prevent burning, until salmon is cooked to desired doneness. Remove from heat and serve immediately.

Otavalo Animal Market, Ecuador
"Maria had a little lamb, little lamb, little lamb..."

plantain crusted red snapper

yield: 4 servings

ingredients

- 1 (5 oz.) bag plantain chips or recipe on pg. 82
- ½ cup gluten free panko or bread crumbs
- 2 tbsp. lemon juice
- 4 (6-8 oz.) red snapper fillets
- salt and freshly ground black pepper to taste
- 1 (1.25 oz.) packet Ortega Taco Seasoning
- 1 large egg mixed with 1 tbsp. water, lightly beaten
- ¼ cup extra-virgin olive oil
- lime wedges (optional)

directions

1. Grind plantain chips and panko or bread crumbs in a blender until you create a smooth flour. Set aside.
2. Pour lemon juice over snapper fillets and season with salt and pepper.
3. In a medium bowl, mix Ortega Taco Seasoning with plantain chip flour. Coat fillets in egg, then toss in crumb mixture. Heat oil until sizzling, add fillets to pan, and cook until golden, about 2-3 minutes on each side.
4. Serve with lime wedges if desired.

rosemary walnut crusted salmon with garlic aioli

yield: 6 servings

ingredients

Garlic Aioli:

- ½ cup mayonnaise or plain yogurt
- 2 garlic cloves, minced
- 1 tbsp. lemon juice
- 1 tsp. Dijon mustard
- salt and freshly ground black pepper to taste

Salmon:

- 3 tbsp. lemon juice
- 6 (6 oz.) salmon fillets
- 2 large eggs
- 2 cups ground walnuts
- 2 tbsp. chopped fresh rosemary or 2 tsp. dried rosemary
- salt and freshly ground black pepper to taste

directions

1. Preheat oven to 350° and grease a baking sheet.
2. To create the garlic aioli, mix mayonnaise or plain yogurt, garlic, lemon juice, mustard, salt, and pepper in a bowl and keep refrigerated until serving.
3. Pour lemon juice over salmon fillets.
4. Beat eggs in a bowl. In a separate bowl or pan, mix ground walnuts, rosemary, salt, and pepper. Dip salmon in egg, then in walnut mixture to coat.
5. Place salmon on baking sheet and bake until salmon is cooked through, about 20 minutes. Serve with chilled garlic aioli on the side.

tuscan tuna steaks with basil yogurt sauce

yield: 4 servings

ingredients

- 4 (8 oz.) fresh tuna steaks, 1-inch thick
- zest of 1 lemon
- 3 tbsp. chopped fresh flat-leaf parsley
- 2 tbsp. chopped fresh rosemary
- 3 garlic cloves, chopped
- salt and freshly ground black pepper to taste
- 3 tbsp. olive oil

Basil Yogurt Sauce:

- 3 tbsp. plain yogurt
- 1 cup fresh basil leaves
- 2 tbsp. chopped roasted red pepper (jarred is fine)
- salt and freshly ground black pepper to taste

directions

1. Rinse and pat tuna steaks dry, then place tuna in a dish.
2. Place lemon zest, parsley, rosemary, garlic, salt, pepper, and oil in a bowl. Whisk ingredients until well combined.
3. Pour mixture onto tuna, coating pieces evenly on each side. Let marinate 10-15 minutes.
4. While tuna is marinating, preheat grill to medium-high heat or set oven to broil. Grill or broil tuna steaks 4-6 minutes on each side depending on whether you prefer the interior pink or well-done. Serve with basil yogurt sauce on top.

Basil Yogurt Sauce:

1. Place yogurt, basil, roasted red pepper, salt, and pepper in a blender and blend until smooth.

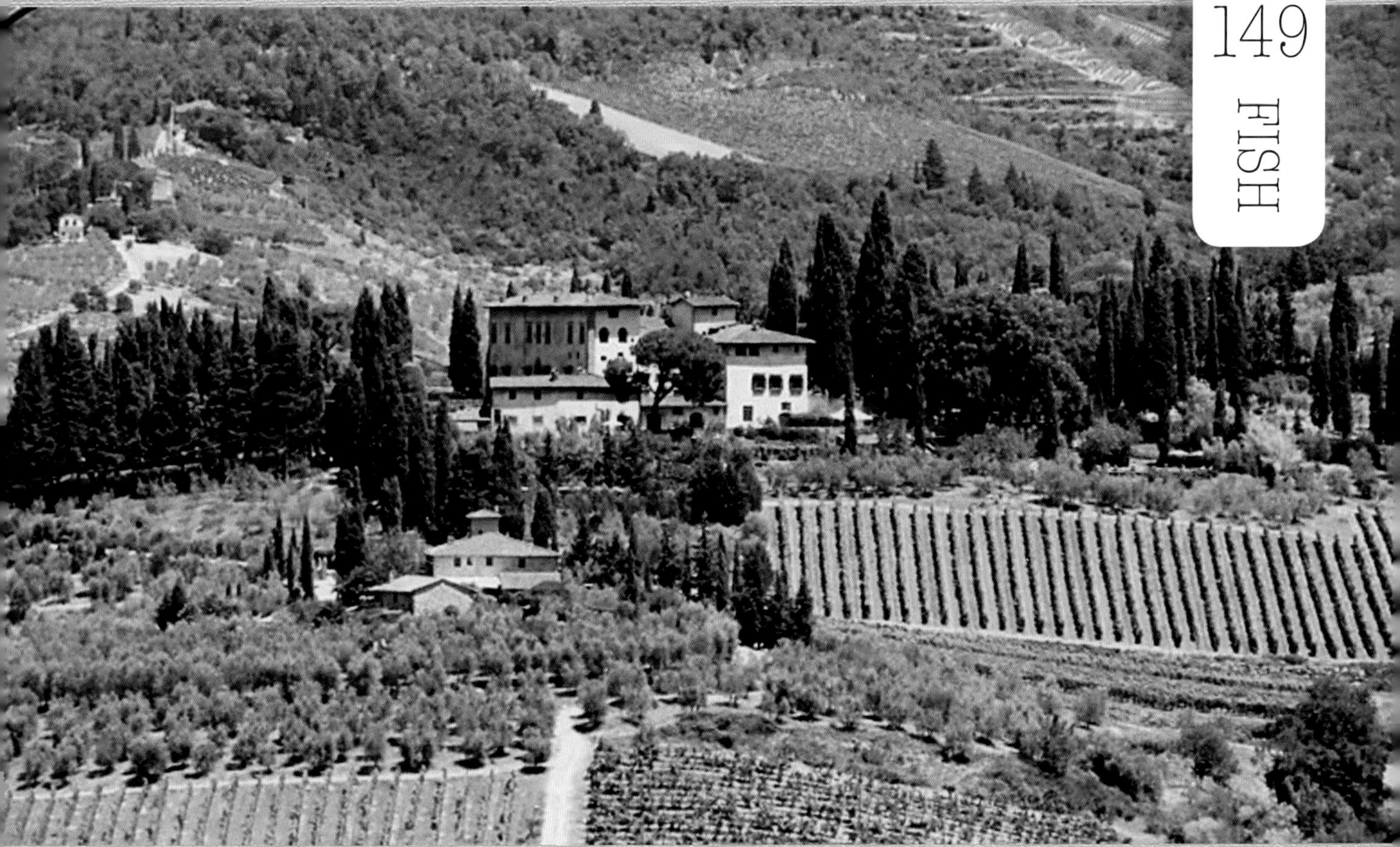

POST CARD

Place
Stamp Here
Domestic
One cent
Foreign
Twocents

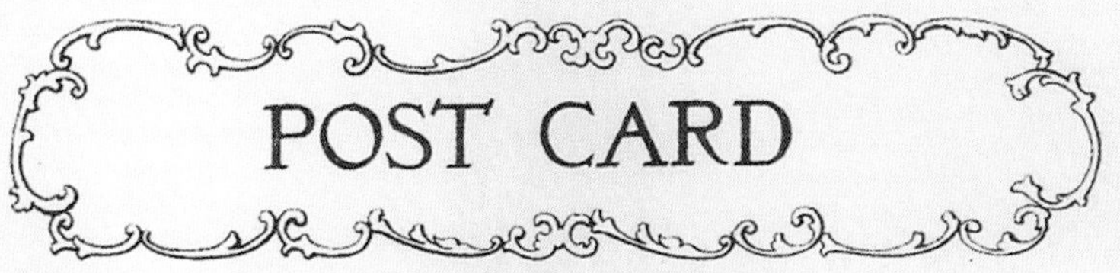

THIS SPACE MAY BE USED FOR WRITING.

Siena,
Tuscany,
Italy

THIS SIDE FOR THE ADDRESS ONLY.

Words can do no justice in describing the breathtaking sight of the rolling hills of Siena, Tuscany. Classic English writers are not remise in their exuberant descriptions of this stunning region.

Poultry

Edinburgh, Scotland
Local sheep enjoying the view in Edinburgh, Scotland.

baked chicken with apple & fennel

yield: 4-6 servings

ingredients

- 2 carrots, peeled and sliced
- 1 small fennel bulb, trimmed, quartered, and cut lengthwise through the core into ½-inch thick wedges
- 1 large yellow onion, diced
- 2 large granny smith apples, unpeeled and diced
- 1 large chicken, cut into eighths
- ½ cup apple juice
- ½ cup chicken stock
- 2 tbsp. Dijon mustard
- 1 tsp. apple cider vinegar
- salt and freshly ground black pepper to taste
- 1 tbsp. chopped fresh tarragon
- 1 tbsp. chopped fresh parsley

directions

1. Preheat oven to 400°.
2. Scatter carrots, fennel, onion, and apples over the bottom of a large roasting pan. Arrange chicken pieces, skin side up, on top of the vegetables.
3. In a small bowl, mix apple juice, stock, mustard, vinegar, salt, and pepper to create dressing. Pour dressing over chicken, then sprinkle with tarragon and parsley.
4. Bake for 1 ½ hours, first hour covered, uncovering for last ½ hour or until skin is golden brown and chicken is cooked through.

Place
Stamp Here
Domestic
One cent
Foreign
Twocents

THIS SPACE MAY BE USED FOR WRITING.

THIS SIDE FOR THE ADDRESS ONLY.

Paris,
France

The three shades
of the Eiffel Tower.
Always magical!

chicken breasts with fig-mustard glaze

yield: 4 servings

ingredients

- 4 (6 oz.) boneless, skinless chicken breast halves
- ¼ tsp. salt
- ¼ tsp. freshly ground black pepper
- 3 tbsp. extra-virgin olive oil
- ½ cup fig preserves
- ¼ cup merlot or other red wine
- 2 tbsp. water
- 2 tbsp. Dijon mustard
- 1 cup halved fresh figs

directions

1. Season chicken with salt and pepper.
2. Coat a large, non-stick skillet with oil. Heat over medium-high heat. Add chicken to pan and cook until chicken is lightly browned, about 8 minutes, turning once halfway through cooking time.
3. While chicken is cooking, combine preserves, wine, water, and mustard. When chicken is almost totally cooked, spoon mixture over chicken in pan. Cover, reduce heat, and simmer until chicken is cooked through, about 5 minutes. Garnish with fresh figs.

chicken tikka masala

(Chicken in a Creamy Tomato Curry)

yield: 4-6 servings

ingredients

- 2 cups tofu sour cream, divided
- 1 tbsp. lemon juice
- 1 tsp. salt, divided
- 4 tsp. ground cumin, divided
- 2 tsp. cayenne pepper
- 2 tsp. freshly ground black pepper
- 1 tsp. ground cinnamon
- 1 tbsp. peeled, minced fresh ginger
- 18 oz. boneless, skinless chicken breasts, cut into bite-sized pieces
- 1 tbsp. olive oil, plus more for coating skewers
- 1 garlic clove, minced
- 1 jalapeño pepper, deseeded, stemmed, and finely chopped
- 2 tsp. paprika
- 1 cup tomato sauce
- ¼ cup chopped fresh cilantro or parsley

directions

1. In a large bowl, combine 1 cup tofu sour cream, lemon juice, ½ tsp. salt, 2 tsp. cumin, cayenne pepper, black pepper, cinnamon, and ginger. Stir in chicken, cover, and refrigerate for 1 hour.
2. Preheat grill or oven to 400°. Thread chicken onto skewers and discard marinade. Be sure to apply a light coat of oil on skewers prior to threading chicken. Place chicken on grill or in oven. Grill until juices run clear, about 5 minutes on each side or roast until cooked through, about 15 minutes.
3. Place a large skillet over medium heat and add oil. Sauté garlic and jalapeño for 1 minute. Season with paprika and the remaining 2 tsp. cumin and ½ tsp. salt. Stir in tomato sauce and the remaining 1 cup tofu sour cream. Simmer over low heat until sauce thickens, about 10-15 minutes. Add chicken and simmer for 5-10 minutes. Garnish with cilantro or parsley.

This is the fourth time I have put off writing a caption for the Taj Mahal because...it's the Taj Mahal in Agra, Uttar Pradesh, India! Cliché or not words can do no justice to this resplendent world wonder.

chicken with mango ginger chutney

yield: 4 servings

ingredients

- 1 tbsp. extra-virgin olive oil
- 1 medium onion, chopped
- 1 garlic clove, minced
- 2 ripe but firm mangos, peeled and cut into ½-inch cubes
- 1 tbsp. peeled, chopped fresh ginger
- a pinch of red pepper flakes
- ½ cup water
- 4 tbsp. granulated sugar or agave nectar
- 6 bone-in, skin on, chicken leg quarters or breasts, trimmed of excess fat

directions

1. Heat oil in a large skillet over medium heat. Add onion and cook, stirring occasionally, until translucent, about 5 minutes. Add garlic and cook 1 minute more, then add mangos, ginger, red pepper flakes, water, and sugar or agave nectar. Bring to a simmer, reduce heat to low, cover, and cook for 30 minutes.
2. Preheat oven to 400°.
3. Place chicken in a 9x13 pan.
4. Once the chutney has thickened, pour over chicken. Bake for about 1 hour and 15 minutes, first hour covered, uncovering for last 15 or until skin is golden brown and chicken is cooked through.

Pushkar, India
This local celebrity, cleverly named, Kicasso, was excited to show off his talent and much to my surprise, also showed me clippings of reviews of his work in prominent Western newspapers.

Angkor Wat, Siem Riep, Cambodia

coconut crusted chicken with plum dipping sauce

yield: 3-4 servings

ingredients

- 2 large eggs
- ½ cup coconut flour or other gluten free flour
- 1 ½ cups packaged unsweetened shredded coconut
- 12 oz. skinless, boneless chicken tenderloins or chicken breasts, sliced into 1-inch thick strips
- 6 tbsp. light extra-virgin olive or canola oil

Plum Dipping Sauce:

- 5 ripe plums, diced, pits discarded
- 3 tbsp. lime juice
- ¼ cup granulated sugar or agave nectar
- ½ tsp. ground cardamom
- ½ tsp. ground cinnamon

directions

1. Beat eggs and set aside.
2. In a separate bowl, combine coconut or other flour and shredded coconut.
3. Dip chicken in egg mixture then cover with coconut breading.
4. Heat oil in a sauté pan over medium heat. Add chicken pieces a few at a time and fry them until cooked through and golden brown, about 3 minutes per side (depending on thickness of chicken).
5. In a small saucepan combine plums, lime juice, and sugar or agave nectar and bring to a boil. Reduce heat and simmer until plums soften, about 10-15 minutes.
6. Let cool then stir in cardamom and cinnamon.
7. Serve chicken at room temperature with plum dipping sauce.

Dambach le Ville, France

coq au vin with saffron quinoa

yield: 2-4 servings

ingredients

- 1 cup uncooked quinoa, rinsed
- salt and freshly ground black pepper to taste
- a pinch of saffron or turmeric
- 2 cups water
- ½ cup mushrooms, thinly sliced
- 4 chicken leg quarters or bone-in breasts
- 3 tbsp. olive oil
- 4 tsp. paprika
- 1 cup dry white wine

directions

1. Preheat oven to 400°.
2. Pour quinoa into a 9x13 pan.
3. Season with salt, pepper, and saffron or turmeric.
4. Pour water on top of quinoa and stir to combine.
5. Sprinkle mushrooms on top of quinoa.
6. Rub chicken with oil, paprika, salt, and pepper and place on top of quinoa in pan.
7. Pour wine on top of chicken.
8. Bake for 1 hour, first 45 minutes covered, uncovering for last 15 minutes or until skin is golden brown and chicken is cooked through.

duck à l'orange

yield: 4 servings

ingredients

- 1 whole 5 lb. duckling
- 4 tsp. paprika
- salt and freshly ground black pepper to taste
- 1 tbsp. olive oil
- 1 (16 oz.) bottle orange marmalade (if the preserves have no zest, add shredded zest from 1 orange)
- 1 cup dry white wine
- ¼ cup balsamic vinegar
- 1 large white onion, chopped

directions

1. Preheat oven to 400° and grease a 9x13 pan.
2. Season duck with paprika, salt, and pepper, then place, skin side up, in pan and drizzle with oil.
3. Mix together marmalade, wine, and vinegar, and pour sauce over duck. Sprinkle with onion.
4. Bake for 1 ½ hours, first hour covered, uncovering for last ½ hour or until skin is golden and chicken is cooked through.

Tip: For a more cost-efficient alternative, substitute duckling with a 5 lb. chicken.

POST CARD

Place Stamp Here
Domestic One cent
Foreign Twocents

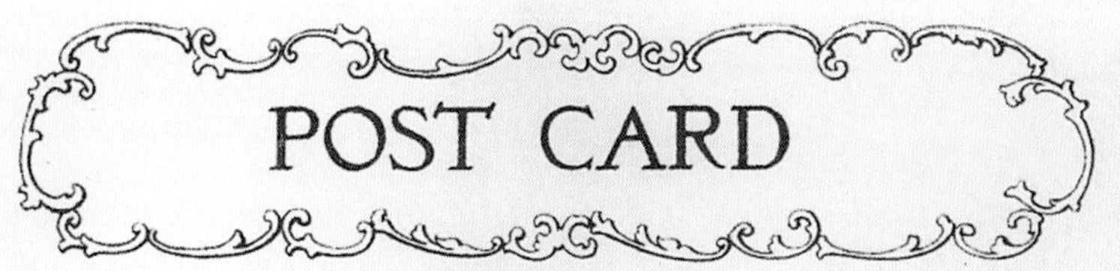

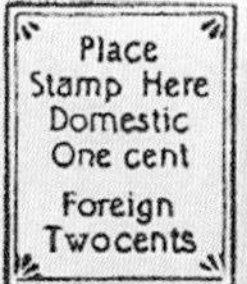

THIS SPACE MAY BE USED FOR WRITING.

Saint Tropez, France

THIS SIDE FOR THE ADDRESS ONLY.

I instantly fell in love with the vibrant pinks and blues, characteristic of the ever charming Côte d'Azur town of Saint-Tropez.

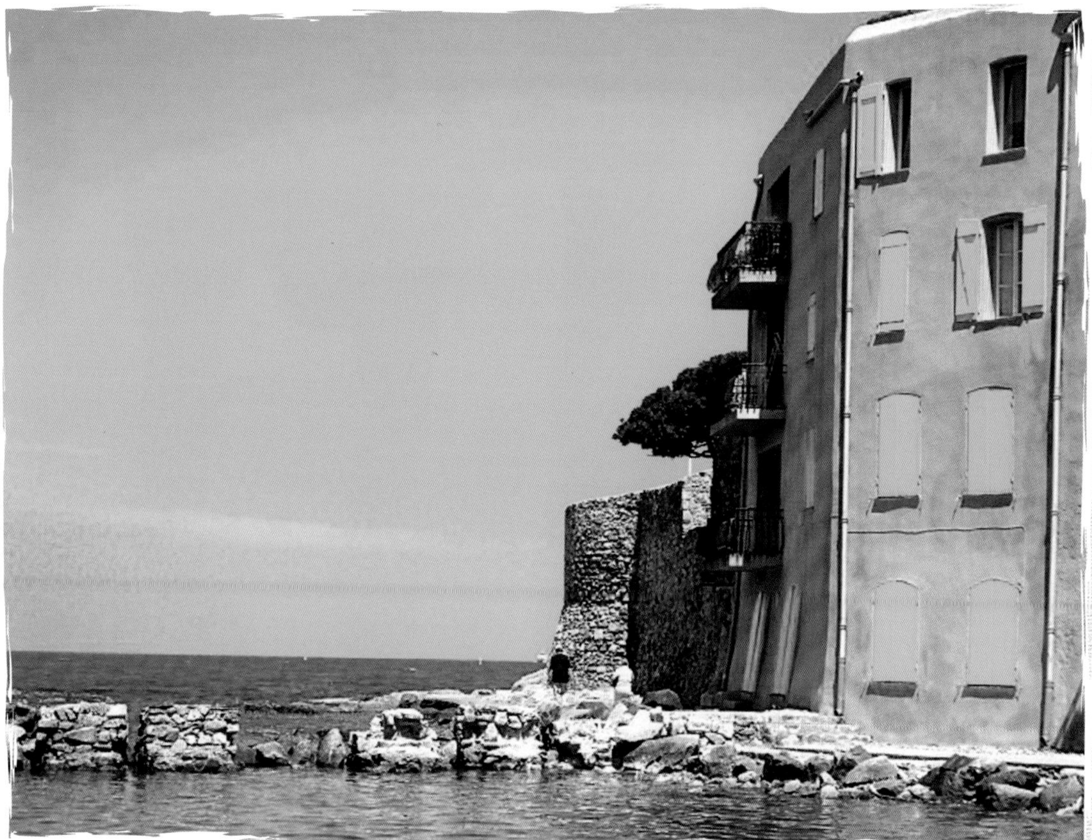

Jaipur, India
Even the camels here are colorful and well dressed.

garlic & almond chicken

yield: 4 servings

ingredients

- 1 tbsp. cornstarch, dissolved in 2 tbsp. cold water
- 4 garlic cloves, chopped
- 2 cups chicken stock
- ⅔ cup dry sherry or white wine
- ½ cup almond butter
- salt and freshly ground black pepper to taste
- ½ tsp. saffron threads or 1 ½ tsp. turmeric (for color)
- 1 tbsp. olive oil
- 4 chicken leg quarters or bone-in breasts
- 1 large white onion, minced
- ¼ cup slivered almonds
- 1 tbsp. chopped fresh flat-leaf parsley

directions

1. Heat a cast iron pot or Dutch oven over medium heat. Add dissolved cornstarch and garlic. Cook, stirring frequently, for 1 minute. Add stock, sherry or wine, almond butter, salt, pepper, and saffron or turmeric. Cook over medium heat for 30 minutes, then remove sauce and set aside.
2. Heat oil in the same pot over medium-high heat. Season chicken with salt and pepper. Add to pot and cook until chicken is golden brown on all sides, about 12 minutes (this step is just to brown the skin). Transfer chicken to a plate.
3. Add onion to pot. Cook, stirring often, until onion is caramelized around edges, about 6 minutes. Return sauce and chicken to pot, pushing chicken down to submerge. Bring sauce to a simmer, cover, and reduce heat to low. Simmer until chicken is cooked through, about 20 minutes. Garnish with almonds and parsley and season with salt and pepper.

Mindo, Ecuador
Not all snowbirds fly to Florida to escape the cold. These two hummingbirds are fighting for some prime real estate here.

grilled chicken with spicy mango salsa

yield: 2 servings

ingredients

Chicken:
- 2 tbsp. honey
- 2 tsp. chopped fresh rosemary or ¾ tsp. crushed dried rosemary
- 2 tsp. ground cumin
- 1 ½ tsp. paprika
- ⅛ tsp. garlic powder
- ⅛ tsp. onion powder
- salt and freshly ground black pepper to taste
- 12 oz. boneless, skinless chicken breasts, cut into strips
- 2 tbsp. olive oil

Spicy Mango Salsa:
- 3 ripe but firm mangos, peeled and diced (if closer to green that's okay too)
- ¼ cup lime juice
- ¼ cup chopped fresh cilantro
- 4 scallions, diced
- 1 small jalapeño, deseeded, stemmed, and minced
- 1 tsp. ground cumin
- ½ tsp. garlic powder
- salt and freshly ground black pepper to taste

directions

1. In a large bowl, combine honey and all seasonings for the chicken.
2. Coat chicken strips lightly in oil. Rub spice mixture onto both sides of chicken strips and return chicken to bowl.
3. Refrigerate chicken for at least 30 minutes to absorb flavors.
4. While chicken is marinating, prepare the salsa by mixing all ingredients in a bowl.
5. To cook the chicken, you can either grill the strips over high heat for about 15 minutes, flipping frequently, or pan-fry them over medium heat for about 5 minutes per side.
6. Once cooked, let chicken sit for 1-2 minutes to allow juices to spread, then serve warm with salsa.

Bridge Festival in Bali, Indonesia

lemongrass chicken skewers

yield: 4 servings

ingredients

- 1 lb. ground chicken
- 2 tbsp. toasted sesame oil
- 2 tbsp. gluten free soy sauce, plus more for dipping
- 2 tbsp. lemon juice
- 1 large egg
- 2 tbsp. gluten free panko or bread crumbs
- 1 bunch of scallions, chopped
- 3 tbsp. extra-virgin olive oil for frying
- 3 lemongrass stalks, cut into 1-2-inch pieces

directions

1. In a large bowl, mix chicken, toasted sesame oil, soy sauce, lemon juice, egg, panko or bread crumbs, and scallions, until well combined. Form 1-inch round "meatballs".
2. Heat a large non-stick skillet with extra-virgin olive oil over medium-high heat. Once oil is hot, add 6-8 "meatballs" at a time and cook until chicken is cooked through, about 2-3 minutes on each side. Set aside. Repeat until all chicken has been cooked.
3. Serve cocktail style, using lemongrass as toothpicks along with your favorite gluten free soy sauce for dipping.

POST CARD

Place Stamp Here
Domestic One cent
Foreign Twocents

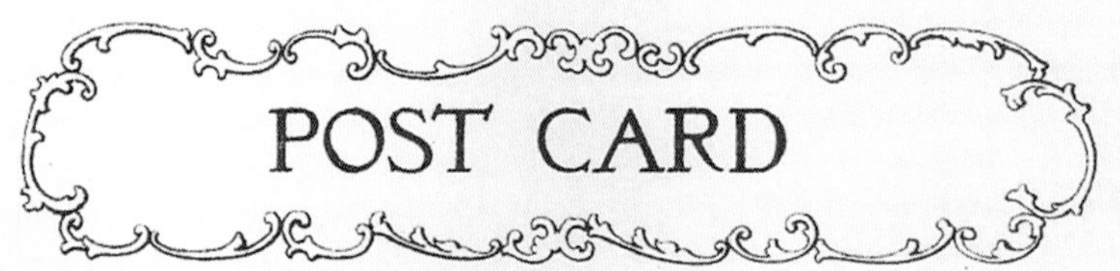

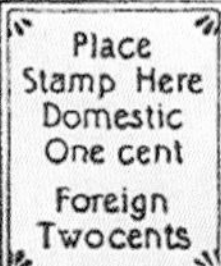

THIS SPACE MAY BE USED FOR WRITING.

Lake Como,
Italy

THIS SIDE FOR THE ADDRESS ONLY.

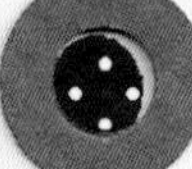

Out stalking George
Clooney on the
beautiful Lake Como.
No, but seriously.

mediterranean chicken

yield: 8 servings

ingredients

- 2 large chickens, cut into eighths or 8 chicken leg quarters
- 1 tbsp. zatar
- paprika, garlic powder, salt, and freshly ground black pepper to taste
- 2 cups sun-dried tomatoes
- 2 cups pitted black, green, or mixed olives
- 2 cups marinated artichokes
- 2 cups frozen whole pearl onions
- 1 tbsp. lemon juice
- 1 tbsp. olive oil

directions

1. Preheat oven to 400°.
2. Sprinkle chicken with zatar, paprika, garlic powder, salt, and pepper.
3. Place chicken in 10x13 pan, skin side up, and cover with sun-dried tomatoes, olives, artichokes, and onions.
4. Drizzle lemon juice and oil over chicken.
5. Cover and bake for 1 ½ hours (for leg quarters, bake only 1 hour).

moroccan chicken

yield: 8 servings

ingredients

- 1 tsp. ground cinnamon
- 1 tsp. turmeric
- 1 tsp. ground cumin
- paprika, garlic powder, salt, and freshly ground black pepper to taste
- 2 tbsp. honey
- 2 tbsp. olive oil
- 2 whole chickens, cut into eighths or 8 chicken leg quarters
- 2 cups pitted black, green, or mixed olives
- 2 cups frozen whole pearl onions
- ½ cup dried apricots
- ¼ cup dried figs
- ¼ cup dried dates

directions

1. Preheat oven to 400°.
2. Mix all spices, honey, and oil in a bowl until combined.
3. Rub chicken all over with mixture from bowl. Place skin side up in a 10x13 pan. Top chicken with olives, onions, apricots, figs, and dates. Drizzle any remaining rub over the ingredients.
4. Bake 1 ½ hours, first hour covered, uncovering for last ½ hour or until skin is golden brown and chicken is cooked through.

POULTRY

nasi goreng

(Indionesian Fried Rice)

yield: 4 servings

ingredients

- 1 cup brown rice
- 2 large eggs
- 3 tbsp. peanut oil, divided
- 12 oz. boneless, skinless chicken breasts, cubed
- 2 large carrots, peeled and diced
- 4 garlic cloves, roughly chopped
- ¼ cup gluten free soy sauce
- 1 red bell pepper, deseeded, stemmed, and diced
- 1 bunch of scallions, chopped

directions

1. Prepare rice according to the directions on the package.
2. While rice is cooking, beat eggs with a fork until well blended. Heat 1 tbsp. oil in a non-stick frying pan, pour in eggs, and cook over low heat until eggs have set. Flip half of eggs to create an omelet. Carefully remove from pan and set aside to cool.
3. Heat the remaining 2 tbsp. oil in a large skillet and add chicken, carrots, and garlic. Stir-fry until chicken is cooked through, about 10 minutes.
4. Add cooked rice, soy sauce, bell pepper, and scallions. Stir-fry until soft, about 10 minutes.
5. When omelet is cool, roll up and slice into very thin strips then add to the top of the stir-fry.

Bali, Indonesia

A native of the Long Neck Hill Tribe in Chaing Mai, Thailand.

pad thai

yield: 4 servings

ingredients

- 4 tbsp. extra-virgin olive oil, divided
- 12 oz. boneless, skinless chicken breasts, cut into strips
- 1 cup rice noodles, soaked to soften and drained
- 2 tbsp. water
- 2 tbsp. tamarind juice or Worcestershire sauce
- 1 tbsp. gluten free soy sauce
- 1 tbsp. chopped fresh cilantro or parsley
- 3 tbsp. ground peanuts
- ½ tsp. chili powder
- 1 tsp. granulated sugar or agave nectar
- 1 cup bean sprouts, tails removed, rinsed well, and drained
- 2 scallions, chopped

Garnish:

- 2 tsp. ground peanuts
- a handful of bean sprouts, tails removed, rinsed well, and drained
- ¼ tsp. chili powder
- lime wedges

directions

1. Heat 2 tbsp. oil in a large skillet over medium heat. Stir-fry chicken, until cooked through, about 7-10 minutes. Remove chicken from pan.
2. Using the same pan, heat the remaining 2 tbsp. oil. Add rice noodles, water, tamarind juice or Worcestershire sauce, soy sauce, cilantro or parsley, peanuts, chili powder, and sugar or agave nectar, and stir-fry for 5-7 minutes. Return chicken to pan, then add bean sprouts and scallions and continue to stir-fry another 4-5 minutes.
3. Garnish with additional peanuts, raw bean sprouts, chili powder, and lime wedges.

pineapple mint chicken

yield: 2-4 servings

ingredients

- ¼ cup olive oil, divided
- 1 tsp. chili powder
- 1 tsp. ground cumin
- salt and freshly ground black pepper to taste
- 12 oz. boneless, skinless chicken breasts, cubed
- 1 large white onion, diced
- 2 cups diced fresh or frozen pineapple
- 1 cup chopped fresh mint

directions

1. Rub chicken with 2 tbsp. oil, then sprinkle with chili powder, cumin, salt, and pepper. Let chicken sit for at least 20 minutes.
2. Heat the remaining 2 tbsp. oil in a large frying pan over medium-high heat. Sauté onion until translucent, about 5 minutes, then add chicken and pineapple. Cook until chicken is cooked through, about 6-7 minutes. Stir in mint and serve.

Bali, Indonesia

tandoori chicken

(Indian Style Grilled Chicken)

yield: 4 servings

ingredients

- 3 tbsp. coconut oil
- 1 tbsp. garam masala
- 1 tbsp. paprika
- 1 tsp. ground coriander
- 1 tsp. ground cumin
- 1 tsp. turmeric
- 1 tsp. cayenne pepper
- 1 cup tofu sour cream
- 2 tbsp. lemon juice
- 4 garlic cloves, minced
- 2 tbsp. peeled, minced fresh ginger
- 1 tsp. salt
- 4 bone-in, skinless chicken leg quarters or breasts
- vegetable oil for grilling

directions

1. Heat coconut oil in a small pan over medium heat. Add garam masala, paprika, coriander, cumin, turmeric, and cayenne pepper, stirring frequently, until spices are fragrant, about 2-3 minutes. Let cool completely.
2. Whisk cooled spice-oil mixture into the tofu sour cream, then mix in lemon juice, garlic, ginger and salt.
3. Score chicken in 3-4 places, then coat in marinade, cover, and refrigerate for 2-24 hours.
4. Rub grill grates with a paper towel soaked in vegetable oil. Prepare grill so that one side is quite hot over direct heat, and the other side cooler, not over direct heat. (If using charcoal, leave one side of the grill without coals, so you have a hot side and a cooler side. If you are using a gas grill, just turn on half the burners.) Remove chicken from marinade and shake off excess. Chicken should be coated thoroughly in marinade, but not dripping excessively. Place chicken on hot side of grill and cover. Cook 2-3 minutes before checking.
5. Turn chicken occasionally so it browns (even a little bit charred) on all sides, then move it to the cool side of the grill. Cover and cook until juices run clear, about 15-20 minutes.

POST CARD
Place Stamp Here Domestic One cent Foreign Twocents
THIS SPACE MAY BE USED FOR WRITING.
THIS SIDE FOR THE ADDRESS ONLY.
Pushkar, India
Pigeons soar to the sound of the drums at this ancient Hindu temple.

Meats

Pushkar, India
Outside her one room home, this artisan makes bracelets to sell in the local bazaar. Indian woman loooove their bangles!

beef korma

(Indian Spiced Braised Beef)

yield: 4-6 servings

ingredients

Meat:
- 2 lbs. beef, cut into cubes (any cut of meat is fine because it is being slow cooked)
- salt and freshly ground black pepper to taste
- 2 tbsp. vegetable oil
- 2 large white onions, diced
- 2 garlic cloves, minced
- 4 ½ cups chicken or beef stock
- 2 tbsp. tomato paste
- 2 tbsp. tamari sauce
- 1 tsp. cracked black pepper
- 1 cup red wine

Sauce:
- 3 tbsp. vegetable oil
- 1 tbsp. chopped fresh cilantro or parsley, plus more for garnish if desired
- 1 tbsp. ground cumin
- 1 tbsp. ground cardamom
- 1 tsp. chili powder
- ½ tsp. ground cloves
- ½ tsp. ground cinnamon
- ½ tsp. garam masala
- 1 tsp. granulated sugar or agave nectar
- salt and freshly ground black pepper to taste
- ½ cup almond milk
- 1 cup tofu sour cream
- ¼ cup almond butter

directions

Meat:
1. Season beef with salt and pepper.
2. Heat oil in a Dutch oven over medium-high heat, then add beef in batches, searing the surfaces. Remove beef and set aside. Add onion and garlic to Dutch oven and sauté until browned but not burned.
3. Return beef to Dutch oven and add stock, tomato paste, tamari sauce, cracked pepper, and wine. Bring to a boil, reduce heat, and simmer over low heat until beef is extremely tender, about 4 hours.

Sauce:
1. Heat oil in a separate pot. Sauté cilantro or parsley, cumin, cardamom, chili powder, ground cloves, cinnamon, garam masala, sugar or agave nectar, salt, and pepper until fragrant, about 2 minutes.
2. Add almond milk, tofu sour cream, and almond butter. Blend thoroughly, mixing until almond butter is fully absorbed.
3. Bring sauce to a boil, then add cooked beef, reduce heat, and simmer for 20 minutes.
4. Garnish with additional cilantro or parsley and almonds if desired.

Quito, Ecuador

beef tacos

ECUADOR
REPÚBLICA DEL ECUADOR

yield: 6 servings

ingredients

- 3 tbsp. olive oil
- 1 large white onion, diced
- 1 garlic clove, minced
- 2 lbs. ground beef
- 1 tsp. salt
- 1 tsp. ground cumin
- 1 tsp. smoked paprika
- ½ tsp. cracked black pepper
- ¼ tsp. ground chipotle
- ¼ cup chopped fresh cilantro or parsley
- 12 (6-inch) corn tortillas, warmed
- salsa, guacamole, and lime juice

directions

1. Heat oil in a large skillet over medium-high heat. Once hot, add onion and garlic and sauté, stirring occasionally, until onion is translucent and garlic is golden brown, about 5 minutes, then add beef, salt, cumin, paprika, cracked pepper, and chipotle. Stir until beef is cooked through, about 7-10 minutes.
2. Once beef is cooked, add cilantro or parsley. Serve with warmed tortillas, your favorite salsa, guacamole, and a squeeze of lime.

Cotopaxi, Ecuador
Don't wait for a lullaby from the guy on the wall
while you're rocking to sleep in this hammock.

fajitas al sombrero

yield: 4-6 servings

ingredients

- 1 ½ lbs. beef skirt steak
- 3 tbsp. lime juice
- 3 tbsp. light extra-virgin olive or canola oil, divided
- 3 garlic cloves, minced
- salt and freshly ground black pepper to taste
- 1 large white onion, thinly sliced
- 1 sweet red pepper, deseeded, stemmed, and thinly sliced
- 1 poblano chili pepper, deseeded, stemmed, and thinly sliced
- 1 tbsp. vegetable oil
- ½ tsp. ground cumin
- ½ tsp. ground coriander
- 6 corn or brown rice tortillas, warmed
- salsa (optional)

directions

1. Place steak in a shallow dish. Drizzle all sides of steak with lime juice and 2 tbsp. light extra-virgin olive or canola oil, then sprinkle with garlic, salt, and pepper. Cover and marinate in the refrigerator for 30 minutes.
2. Set oven to broil. Remove steaks from marinade and pat dry with paper towels. Lightly coat a large skillet with the remaining 1 tbsp. light extra-virgin olive or canola oil. Cook until slightly pink in the center, about 8 minutes, turning once halfway through cooking time. Transfer steak to a cutting board and let cool for about 10 minutes, then thinly slice steak strips against the grain.
3. Meanwhile, in a large bowl, combine onion, sweet red pepper, and poblano chili pepper. Add vegetable oil, tossing to coat; stir in cumin and coriander. Preheat oven broiler. Spread vegetable mixture on a large baking sheet, then broil 4-5-inches from heat until skins are blistered on one side, about 4 minutes, then flip and cook an additional 4 minutes. Remove from oven and set aside.
4. Combine beef and vegetables. Serve with warmed corn or brown rice tortillas and salsa if desired.

let's cook: filet mignon with fresh herb & garlic rub

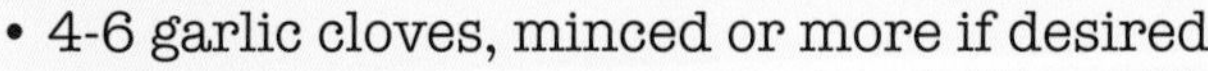

ingredients: **yield:** 4 servings

- 4-6 garlic cloves, minced or more if desired
- 2 tsp. minced fresh basil
- 2 tsp. minced fresh thyme
- 2 tsp. minced fresh rosemary
- ½ tsp. salt
- ¼ tsp. freshly ground black pepper
- 4 (4 oz.) beef tenderloin steaks, 1-inch thick
- ¼ cup olive oil

directions:

1. Combine garlic, basil, thyme, rosemary, salt, and pepper. Rub evenly over steaks.
2. In a large non-stick skillet, heat oil over medium-high heat.
3. Add steaks to pan and cook 4 minutes on each side or until cooked to desired doneness.

Rosheim, France
Fresh herbs being sold at the farmer's market in Rosheim.

keema

(Indian Style Ground Meat)

yield: 4 servings

ingredients

- 3 tbsp. olive oil, divided
- 1 ½ lbs. ground lamb or beef
- 1 large white onion, finely chopped
- 1 sweet green pepper, deseeded, stemmed, and diced
- 2 garlic cloves, minced
- 1 tbsp. garam masala
- 1 tsp. salt
- 4 tsp. tomato paste
- ¾ cup beef stock
- 1 tbsp. chopped fresh cilantro
- 1 tbsp. chopped fresh parsley
- cooked rice (optional)

directions

1. Heat 2 tbsp. oil in a heavy skillet over high heat. Add meat and cook until evenly brown, stirring often. While cooking, break meat apart with a wooden spoon until crumbled. Drain fat, then transfer cooked meat to a bowl.
2. Using the same skillet, heat the remaining 1 tbsp. oil over medium-high heat and sauté onion until translucent, about 5 minutes. Add sweet green pepper and garlic and sauté until pepper is soft, about 2 minutes. Stir in garam masala and salt and cook for an additional minute.
3. Return browned meat to skillet, then stir in tomato paste and stock until evenly combined. Garnish with cilantro and parsley and serve over rice if desired.

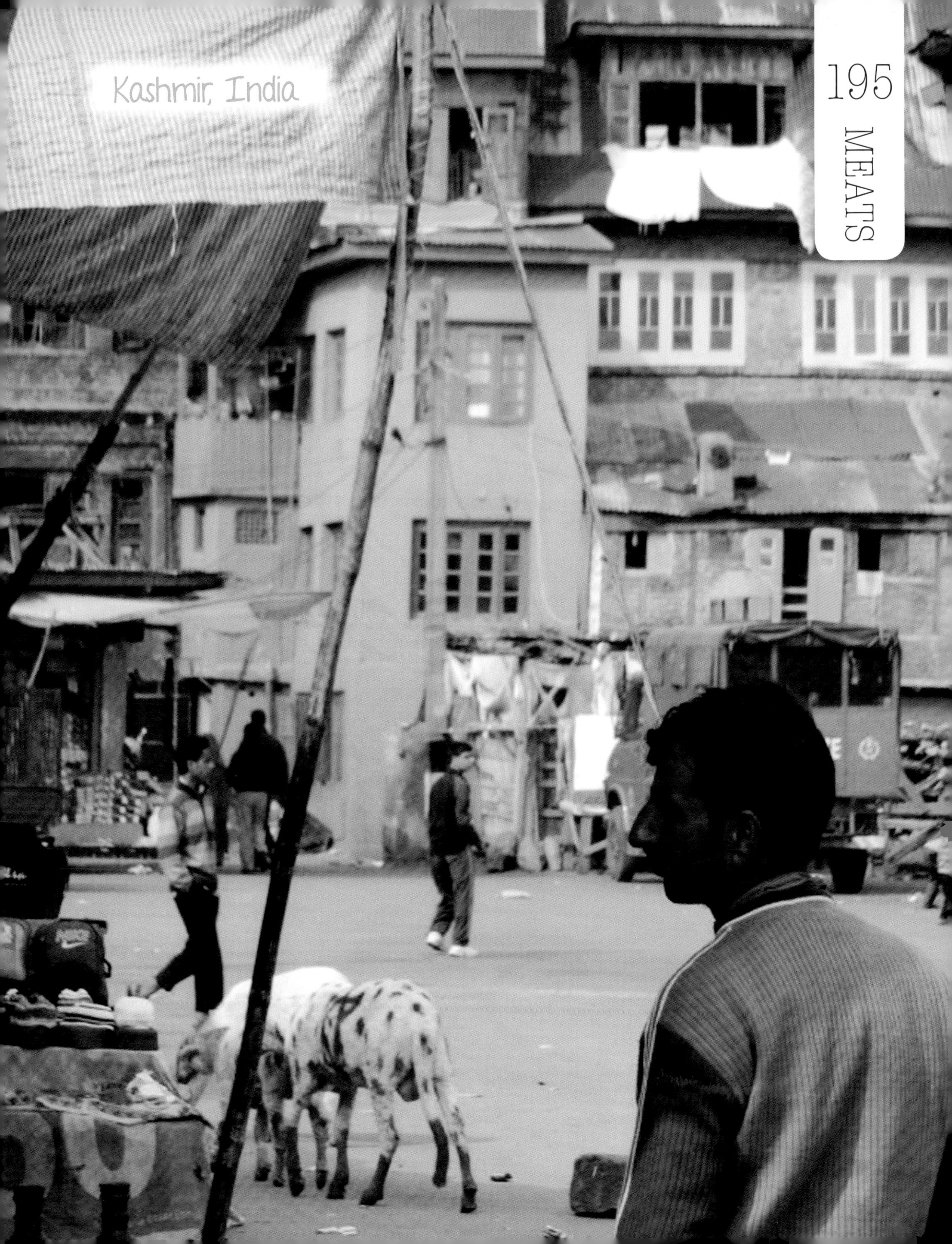
Kashmir, India

Sonamarg, India
This mother gives a whole new meaning to multitasking while washing her dishes along with her children.

DATE No.

lamb curry

yield: 6 servings

ingredients

- 4 tbsp. vegetable oil, divided, plus more if needed
- 2 lbs. lamb stew meat, cut into cubes
- 1 large white onion, chopped
- 2 tbsp. ground coriander
- 1 tbsp. ground cardamom
- 1 ½ tsp. ground cumin
- 1 tsp. ground ginger
- 1 tsp. turmeric
- ½ tsp. garlic powder
- ¼ tsp. cayenne pepper or more if desired
- 2 cups beef stock
- salt and freshly ground black pepper to taste
- ¼ cup tofu sour cream
- 1 tsp. lemon juice

INDIA

directions

1. Heat 2 tbsp. oil in a medium stock pot over medium-high heat. Cook lamb in batches until browned on all sides, using additional oil as necessary, about 3 minutes per batch. Remove lamb and set aside.
2. Heat the remaining 2 tbsp. oil in the stock pot over medium-high heat. Stir in onion and cook until translucent, about 5 minutes. Add coriander, cardamom, cumin, ginger, turmeric, garlic powder, and cayenne pepper; cook and stir until spices are fragrant, about 2 minutes.
3. Return lamb to stock pot, pour in stock, and season with salt and pepper. Bring to a boil over high heat, then reduce heat to low, cover, and simmer until lamb is very tender, about 1 hour.
4. Once lamb is very tender, remove stock pot lid, and cook until sauce thickens slightly, about 20 minutes. Stir in tofu sour cream and lemon juice before serving.

Scenes from the famous painter Claude Monet's garden in Giverny, France.

pistachio mint crusted rack of lamb

yield: 6 servings

ingredients

- 2 racks of lamb (8 bones each), trimmed and frenched
- salt and freshly ground black pepper to taste
- ¼ cup olive oil, divided
- ½ cup shelled pistachios
- 3 cups fresh mint leaves
- 3 peeled garlic cloves
- zest and juice of 1 lemon

directions

1. Preheat oven to 450°.
2. Season lamb generously on all sides with salt and pepper.
3. Heat 1 tbsp. oil in a frying pan or ovenproof skillet over medium-high heat. Once oil is hot, sear lamb on all sides, about 2 minutes per side. Set lamb aside to partially cool.
4. While lamb cools, put pistachios in a food processor and pulse a few times to grind them. Add the remaining 3 tbsp. oil, mint, garlic, lemon zest, and lemon juice. Process until it turns into a pesto.
5. Rub pesto all over lamb. Place lamb in either a 9x13 roasting pan or back in the ovenproof skillet, bone-side down, then place in oven.
6. Roast for 20 minutes for medium-rare or 25 minutes for medium depending on desired doneness. Cover lamb with foil and allow to sit for 10 minutes before cutting into chops. Use a sharp, thin knife to carve.

plum & ginger brisket

yield: 6-8 servings

ingredients

- 4 fresh plums, quartered, pits discarded
- ¼ cup water
- 2 tbsp. rice vinegar
- ¼ cup gluten free soy sauce
- 3-4 garlic cloves, minced
- 1 large white onion, diced
- 1 tbsp. peeled, minced fresh ginger
- 2 tbsp. granulated sugar or agave nectar
- 3 tbsp. toasted sesame oil
- 3 tbsp. extra-virgin olive oil
- 5 lbs. brisket

directions

1. Preheat oven to 350°.
2. Place plums and water in a medium saucepan, bring to a boil, then cook at a simmer, stirring constantly, until a purée-like consistency forms, about 30 minutes.
3. Add vinegar, soy sauce, garlic, onion, ginger, sugar or agave nectar, and toasted sesame oil and stir to combine. Remove from heat.
4. Heat extra-virgin olive oil in a Dutch oven over high heat. Add brisket and cook for 2 minutes on each side. Pour sauce over brisket. Cover and bake for 4 hours or until brisket is soft.

Chiang Mai, Thailand

POST CARD

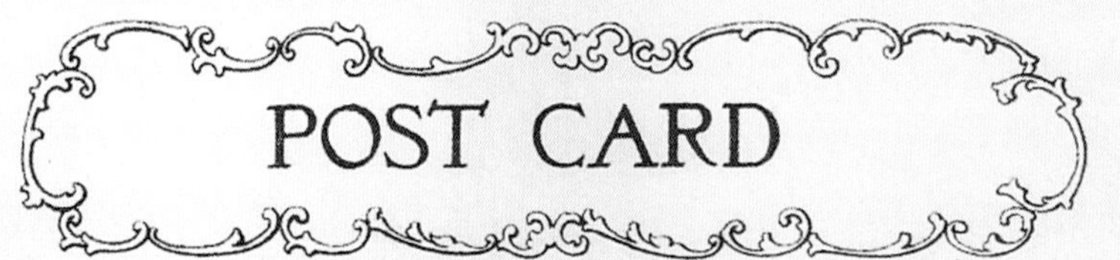

Place Stamp Here
Domestic One cent
Foreign Twocents

THIS SPACE MAY BE USED FOR WRITING.

Rome,
Italy

THIS SIDE FOR THE ADDRESS ONLY.

Sailors enjoying their
day off at beautiful
Piazza Navona

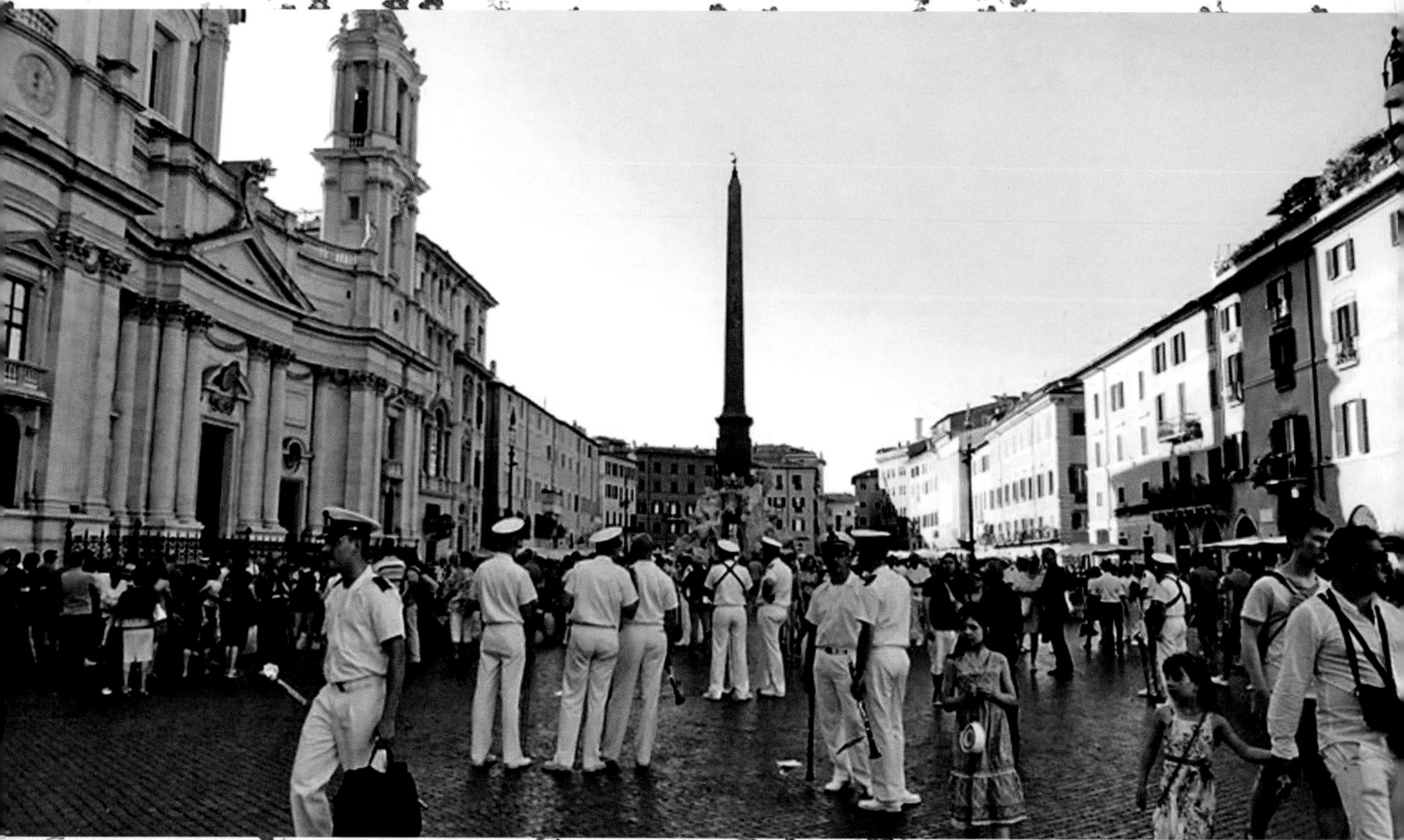

rosemary lamb skewers

yield: 4 servings

ingredients

- 1 lb. boneless lamb, trimmed of all fat and cut into 2-inch cubes
- ½ cup lemon juice
- 10-15 garlic cloves, chopped
- ½ cup olive oil, plus more for coating skewers and vegetables
- 1 tsp. salt
- 1 tsp. freshly ground black pepper
- 1 tbsp. chopped fresh rosemary
- 2 medium yellow onions, cut into eighths
- 2 assorted bell peppers, deseeded, stemmed, and cut into 1-inch pieces

directions

1. In a bowl, combine lamb, lemon juice, garlic, oil, salt, pepper, and rosemary. Marinate in the refrigerator for at least 2-3 hours or up to 48 hours prior to cooking.
2. Thread marinated lamb onto skewers (about 6 cubes per skewer). Be sure to apply a light coat of oil on the skewers prior to threading lamb.
3. Lightly oil onions and peppers then place them on separate skewers, alternating type of vegetable.

   Note: The meat and veggies are cooked on different skewers because the meat will take longer to cook.

4. Cook lamb skewers on grill or under broiler until cooked to desired doneness, about 10-12 minutes, turning once halfway through cooking time.
5. Cook vegetable skewers for 4 minutes, turning once halfway through cooking time. Vegetables should be crisp, yet tender. Be careful not to overcook.

Red rock adventures in
Sedona, Arizona, USA.

southwestern meatballs

yield: 8-10 servings

ingredients

Sauce:

- 1 (16 oz.) jar salsa (mild or spicy, depending on preference)
- 1 (12 oz.) jar dark fruit jam (grape, blueberry, or black currant)
- ¼ cup ketchup
- 1 cup water
- ¼ cup granulated sugar or agave nectar
- salt and freshly groundblack pepper to taste

Meatballs:

- 2 lbs. ground beef
- 2 large eggs
- 1 tbsp. ketchup
- 2 tsp. lemon juice
- 3 tbsp. gluten free panko or bread crumbs
- 1 tbsp. chopped fresh parsley

directions

1. To create the sauce, mix salsa, jam, ketchup, water, sugar or agave nectar, salt, and pepper in a large pot and bring to a boil, then lower heat to a simmer.
2. Combine beef, eggs, ketchup, lemon juice, panko or bread crumbs, and parsley and form into 1-inch round meatballs. Add to sauce.
3. Cover and cook over medium heat until meatballs are cooked through, about 35 minutes.

Paris, France
Scenes of a Parisian ballet.

truffled mushroom silver tip roast

yield: 8 servings

ingredients

- 5 lbs. silver tip roast
- 2 tbsp. olive oil
- 1 tbsp. paprika
- 3-4 garlic cloves, chopped
- ¼ tsp. salt
- ¼ tsp. freshly ground black pepper
- 1 large white onion, diced
- 2 cups dry red wine

Mushroom Sauce:

- 10 assorted mushrooms, thinly sliced
- ½ cup dry red wine
- 5 tbsp. almond milk
- 2 tbsp. olive oil
- 1 tbsp. truffle oil
- salt and freshly ground black pepper to taste
- 1 tbsp. chopped fresh parsley

directions

1. Preheat oven to 350°.
2. Rub roast with 2 tbsp. oil, then sprinkle with paprika, garlic, salt, and pepper.
3. Place roast in a Dutch oven and sear on both sides, then add onion and the 2 cups wine.
4. Cover and roast in oven until tender, about 4 hours.
5. Meanwhile in a large pan, cook mushrooms, ½ cup wine, almond milk, 2 tbsp. olive oil, and truffle oil for five minutes over medium heat, stirring occasionally. Season with salt, pepper, and parsley.
6. When roast is done, pour mushroom sauce on top of roast and let sit for at least 15 minutes before serving.

Desserts

Dublin, Ireland

bailey's irish mousse

yield: 6-8 servings

ingredients

- 3 (8 oz.) packages cream cheese, at room temperature
- ⅓ cup granulated sugar
- ½ cup Bailey's Irish Cream liqueur
- 1 cup semisweet chocolate chips
- 2 cups fully whipped cream, plus more for garnish
- 10-12 gluten free chocolate chip cookies, crushed

directions

1. In a bowl, beat cream cheese and sugar until smooth. Add liqueur and beat until blended.
2. Place chocolate chips in a microwave safe bowl and microwave in 30 second increments until fully melted.
3. Using a rubber spatula combine melted chocolate, cream cheese mixture, and whipped cream. Fold together until evenly combined.
4. Spoon into small dessert dishes or glasses.
5. Allow mousse to chill in the refrigerator for at least 2 hours or overnight before serving. Top with cookies and additional whipped cream.

banana walnut cake

yield: 12 servings

ingredients

- 1 (15 oz.) box gluten free yellow cake mix
- 1 cup milk or almond milk
- 2 large eggs
- ½ cup vegetable oil
- 2-3 ripe bananas, roughly cut into pieces
- 1 tsp. ground cinnamon
- 1 tsp. pure vanilla extract
- 2 cups walnuts, chopped

directions

1. Preheat oven to 350° and grease a 10-inch round baking pan.
2. Empty yellow cake mix into a large mixing bowl. Add milk or almond milk, eggs, oil, bananas, cinnamon, and vanilla. Beat with an electric mixer on medium speed, until evenly combined, about 5 minutes.
3. Spread batter evenly in the prepared pan and top with walnuts.
4. Bake until toothpick inserted in center comes out clean, about 45 minutes. Let cool for 15 minutes before serving.

"Mr. Peck...Drive...!!!" That's a direct quote from me yelling at the driver as I'm sprinting from this local jungle banana lady who was chasing me with her machete.

Notting Hill, London, England
Georgian doors! All these doors were on separate houses all on the same block.

blueberry crumble

yield: 20-24 servings

ingredients

Blueberry Filling:
- 6 cups fresh blueberries
- ⅓ cup granulated sugar
- juice of 2 lemons

Crust and Crumb Topping:
- 1 (15 oz.) box gluten free yellow cake mix
- 2 cups walnuts, finely chopped
- ¾ cup granulated sugar
- ¼ cup brown sugar
- 1 tsp. baking powder
- ¼ tsp. salt
- zest of 1 lemon
- 1 stick (½ cup) unsalted butter, melted
- 1 large egg

directions

1. Preheat oven to 375° and grease a 9x13 pan.
2. Combine blueberry filling ingredients. Mix well and set aside.
3. In a separate bowl mix together cake mix, walnuts, granulated sugar, brown sugar, baking powder, salt, and lemon zest until well combined.
4. Add butter and egg and blend together.
5. Place half the crust mixture into the prepared pan and press it firmly into the bottom. Spoon the blueberry mixture into the crust, being careful not to add too much of the liquid.
6. Using your hands, crumble the rest of the crust mixture over the blueberries so that it is evenly distributed. Bake until crumb topping is light golden brown, about 50 minutes.
7. Let cool for at least 30 minutes before cutting. Cut into 20-24 squares. This dish is best served warm. (Any leftovers should be stored in the refrigerator.)

I'm a postcard fanatic and this is my favorite one! I refused to get on the plane without this souvenir in my possession... you're welcome!

chocolate mousse pie

yield: 6 servings

ingredients

- 12-14 gluten free chocolate chip cookies, crushed
- 2 tbsp. unsalted butter, melted
- ¼ cup granulated sugar
- 2 large eggs
- 1 cup semisweet chocolate chips
- 1 cup fully whipped cream, plus more for garnish
- ½ cup chocolate, shaved

directions

1. In a medium bowl, combine cookies and butter. Using your hands, press the mixture into a 9-inch pie dish.
2. Using an electric mixer, whip sugar and eggs until thick, fluffy, and fully blended.
3. Place chocolate chips in a microwave safe bowl and microwave in 30 second increments until fully melted.
4. Using a spatula, fold melted chocolate into the bowl with the sugar and eggs. Gently fold whipped cream into the mixture and pour the mixture into the piecrust.
5. Refrigerate overnight and decorate with additional whipped cream and shaved chocolate before serving.

churros

yield: 10 churros

ingredients

- ¼ cup granulated sugar
- ¾ tsp. ground cinnamon
- 1 cup water
- ⅓ cup unsalted butter
- 2 tbsp. brown sugar
- ½ tsp. salt
- 1 cup gluten free all-purpose flour
- 1 large egg
- ½ tsp. pure vanilla extract
- canola oil for frying
- confectioners' sugar

directions

1. In a medium bowl, combine granulated sugar and cinnamon. Set aside for topping.
2. In a medium saucepan, combine water, butter, brown sugar, and salt. Bring to a boil over medium heat. Add flour all at once, stirring vigorously with a wooden spoon. Cook and stir until the mixture forms a ball and pulls away from the sides of the pan. Remove from heat and let cool.
3. Line a baking sheet with greased parchment paper. After the dough has cooled for 10 minutes, add egg and vanilla to the saucepan, and beat ingredients well with a wooden spoon to blend them completely. Transfer the mixture to a decorating bag fitted with a large star tip. Pipe 4-inch lengths onto the prepared baking sheet.
4. Heat 3-inches oil in a deep saucepan over medium-high heat. Fry a few strips at a time in hot oil (at least 375°), turning once, until golden brown on all sides, about 5 minutes. Drain on paper towels. Roll warm churros in the cinnamon-sugar mixture to coat. Serve warm

Cotopaxi, Ecuador
This tranquil scene might look primitive at first glance, but check out that sophisticated recycling system! Ecuador? Or California?

Montmartre, Paris, France

Enjoying the view of Montmartre as my fellow artists before me have done for generations past. Shout out to my boyz Monet, Picasso, Modigliani, and Dalí – wish you were here!

classic crème brûlée

yield: 4 servings

ingredients

- 10 tbsp. granulated sugar, divided
- 2 cups heavy cream
- 6 large egg yolks
- 1 tsp. pure vanilla extract

directions

1. Preheat oven to 350˚.
2. Whisk together 6 tbsp. sugar and heavy cream in a microwave safe bowl until well combined. Heat the mixture in the microwave until warm, about 1-2 minutes, and whisk again to dissolve sugar.
3. Whisk in egg yolks and vanilla until smooth.
4. Pour cream mixture into 4 ramekins. Set ramekins into a roasting pan and pour in enough hot water to reach halfway up the sides of the ramekins.
5. Bake until the outer sides are set, but the center is still soft, about 10-15 minutes. Remove ramekins from hot water and chill in the refrigerator for at least 2 hours before caramelizing.
6. Sprinkle 1 tbsp. sugar evenly over the top of each dessert. Use a kitchen torch to lightly toast and melt the sugar topping until brown and bubbly, about 30 seconds. Allow to cool 1-2 minutes, then serve.

An alternate caramelizing method:

Above is the classic method to glazing a Crème Brûlée, however, as a kitchen torch is not a staple in most homes, you may instead set your oven to broil, put your rack on the top shelf, and let the oven get nice and hot. Once the oven is hot, fill an oven safe dish with crushed ice and water and place the ramekins into the ice water bath; broil 3-5 minutes. The cold bath should keep the custard from cooking, but the sugar on top will heat until it caramelizes. Whether using a kitchen torch or broiler, allow sugar topping to cool before serving.

let's cook: coconut cream parfait

ingredients: **yield:** 12-16 servings

- 2 packages instant gluten free vanilla pudding mix
- 1 cup packaged sweetened shredded coconut, plus more for garnish
- 4 cups macaroons or other gluten free cookies
- fully whipped cream
- fresh fruit (optional)

directions:

1. In a bowl, prepare pudding according to the directions on the package. Once pudding has set, mix in coconut.
2. In a separate bowl, crumble macaroons. Using dessert containers of choice, alternate layers of crumbled macaroons and pudding to create layers as you would with a lasagna.
3. Top with additional coconut, whipped cream, and fresh fruit if desired.

Tip: A 4 oz. Mason jar makes a nice and trendy single serving!

coconut sticky rice with mango

yield: 3-5 servings

ingredients

- 1 cup uncooked sushi rice
- 1 cup coconut milk
- ¼ cup coconut water
- 3 tbsp. granulated sugar
- 1 tbsp. salt
- 1 tsp. roasted black sesame seeds (optional)
- 1 tbsp. packaged sweetened shredded coconut
- 3-4 ripe mangos, peeled and sliced

directions

1. Rinse rice in cold water until water runs clear. Cook rice according to the directions on the package, stirring often.
2. During the last 5 minutes the rice cooking, combine coconut milk, coconut water sugar, and salt in a small saucepan. Bring to a boil over low heat, then cook for 2-3 minutes. (Be sure not to let the sauce boil over.)
3. Pour coconut milk mixture over rice and quickly stir. Place over medium-low heat and allow rice to simmer about 15 minutes, stirring every few minutes so as to prevent rice from sticking to the pan and burning. Once sauce is mostly absorbed, remove from heat and allow to cool for 15-20 minutes.
4. Using an ice cream scoop or regular tablespoon, shape rice into golf-sized balls. Sprinkle with sesame seeds, if using, and shredded coconut. Serve warm or at room temperature with mango.

Hanoi, Vietnam

IRISH APPLES
Var. 'ELSTAR'
3€/kg
Value Bag
€4

irish apple cake

yield: 12 servings

ingredients

- 4 tbsp. butter, softened, preferably Irish butter
- ½ cup granulated sugar
- 5 large eggs, beaten
- 1 cup milk
- 4 Granny Smith apples, cored, peeled, and diced
- 1 tsp. pure vanilla extract
- 1 cup coconut flour
- 1 cup almond flour
- 1 tsp. baking powder
- 1 tsp. baking soda
- 1 tsp. ground cinnamon
- vanilla ice cream or fully whipped cream (optional)

directions

1. Preheat oven to 350° and grease an 8-inch square baking pan.
2. In a large bowl, using an electric mixer, cream the butter, sugar, and eggs until light and fluffy.
3. Add milk, apples, and vanilla. Using a spatula, mix until apples are evenly coated.
4. Sift together coconut flour, almond flour, baking powder, baking soda, and cinnamon and add to the wet apple mixture and mix well.
5. Pour batter into the prepared pan and bake until cake is slightly browned and a toothpick inserted into the center comes out clean, about 45 minutes.
6. Remove from oven and allow to cool for 15-30 minutes. Serve with vanilla ice cream or whipped cream if desired.

lemon meringue tart

yield: 10-12 servings

ingredients

Crust:

- 1 ½ cups gluten free all-purpose flour
- a pinch of salt
- 1 stick (½ cup) unsalted butter, room temperature
- ¼ cup granulated sugar
- 1 large egg, lightly beaten
- ½ tsp. pure vanilla extract

Lemon Filling:

- 3 large eggs
- ¾ cup granulated sugar
- ⅓ cup lemon juice
- 4 tbsp. unsalted butter, room temperature, cut into chunks
- 1 tbsp. lemon zest

Meringue:

- 4 large egg whites
- ½ tsp. cream of tartar
- ½ tsp. pure vanilla extract
- ½ cup granulated sugar

Saint Tropez, France

directions

1. To create the crust, sift flour and salt together in a bowl, then set aside. Place butter in an electric mixer and beat until soft, then add sugar and beat until light and fluffy. Slowly add egg and beat until thoroughly combined. Add flour all at once and mix just until combined.
2. Flatten dough into a disk, cover with plastic wrap, and chill in the refrigerator for 30 minutes.
3. Grease an 8-9-inch false bottom tart pan. Press the dough into the pan, making sure the dough is evenly distributed throughout the bottom and up the sides. Prick the bottom of the dough with the tines of a fork and allow to chill in the refrigerator for 20 minutes.
4. Preheat oven to 400˚. Line unbaked crust with foil and fill evenly, to the top with beans or rice. Bake until lightly browned, 20-25 minutes. Remove from oven and let cool.
5. While crust is baking make the lemon filling. Place a metal bowel over a saucepan of simmering water over medium heat. In the metal bowl, whisk together eggs, sugar, and lemon juice until well blended. Whisk constantly, until thick and pale in color, about 10 minutes. Remove from heat and whisk in butter pieces until they are melted and blended in completely. Stir in lemon zest and pour the mixture immediately into baked crust.
6. Reduce oven heat to 350˚. Bake tart until filling is firm but still wobbly towards the center, about 10 minutes.
7. Meanwhile, to create the meringue, use an electric mixer to whisk egg whites until foamy. Add cream of tartar and vanilla and continue beating until soft peaks form. Slowly add sugar and continue to whisk until stiff peaks form.
8. Using a spatula, pour meringue over the entire surface of the hot tart. Cover right up to the crust making sure there are no gaps. Using the back of a spoon, swirl meringue into decorative peaks. Return tart to oven until lightly browned, 10-15 minutes.
9. Allow to cool, then serve. (Any leftovers should be stored in the refrigerator.)

San Gimiginano, Italy

tiramisu

yield: 16-20 servings

ingredients

- 2 (15 oz.) boxes gluten free yellow or sponge cake mix
- 6 large egg yolks
- 1 cup granulated sugar
- 1 ¼ cups mascarpone cheese
- 1 ¾ cups heavy cream
- ½ cup cold espresso
- ¼ cup coffee flavored liqueur, such as Kahlua
- 1 tbsp. cocoa powder

directions

1. Preheat oven to 350° and grease two 8-10-inch round pans. Line the pan bottoms with parchment paper and grease the paper.
2. Make cakes according to the directions on the package. Distribute batter evenly between the pans and bake until toothpick inserted in center comes out clean, about 25 minutes. Remove from oven and let cakes cool for 10 minutes, then remove from pans, remove parchment paper, and place on a cooling rack. Allow to cool completely. Set aside.
3. Whisk egg yolks and sugar in the top of a double boiler over boiling water. Reduce heat to low and cook for about 10 minutes, whisking constantly, making sure the sugar is no longer grainy in texture. Remove from heat and using an electric mixer on medium speed, whip the mixture until it is thick and lemon colored, about 5 minutes. Add mascarpone to whipped yolk mixture, beating until combined.
4. In a separate bowl, using an electric mixer on medium speed, whip heavy cream until stiff peaks form, about 5-7 minutes. Gently fold whipped cream into the mascarpone mixture and set aside.
5. Mix cold espresso with coffee liqueur and set aside.
6. Place the first of the cakes on a plate. Spoon some of the espresso mixture over the cake, allowing the cake to absorb the mixture until moist. Then spoon the cream mixture over the cake, completing the first layer. Repeat to create a second layer, then sift cocoa powder over cake top. Serve chilled.

"·" at end of title/description represents vegetarian options

index

- 4 Bean & Kale Super Stew · 27
- almonds
  - Garlic & Almond Chicken 167
  - Quinoa Veggie Biryani · 120
- Aloo Gobi · 99
- American
  - Coconut Cream Parfait · 222
  - Lemon Ricotta Pancakes · 19
  - Maple Ginger Roasted Sweet Potatoes · 76
  - Onion Lover's Spinach Scramble · 20
  - Pomegranate & Goat Cheese Salad · 53
  - Southwesten Meatballs 205
- apples
  - Baked Chicken with Apple & Fennel 153
  - Irish Apple Cake · 227
- apricots
  - Candied Fig & Goat Cheese Salad · 33
  - Moroccan Chicken 174
- arugula
  - Pasta with Spinach & Arugula Pesto · 118
- avocados
  - Feta Cheese & Quinoa Salad · 41
  - Mandarin Orange Chicken Salad 46
- Baby Bok Choy with Garlic & Ginger · 61
- Bailey's Irish Mousse · 211
- Baked Chicken with Apple & Fennel 153
- Banana Walnut Cake · 212
- basil
  - Eggplant Risotto · 111
  - Garlic & Basil Spaghetti Squash · 112
  - Pasta with Spinach & Arugula Pesto · 118
  - Tuna Steaks ... Basil Yogurt Sauce 148
- beans
  - 4 Bean & Kale Super Stew · 27
  - Black Bean and Corn Salad · 31
  - Tofu in Black Bean Sauce · 126
- beef
  - Beef Korma 187
  - Beef Pho 28
  - Beef Tacos 189
  - Fajitas al Sombrero 191
  - Filet Mignon ... Herb & Garlic Rub 192
  - Irish Blue Potato Beef Stew 43
  - Italian Wedding Soup 45
  - Keema 194
  - Pepper Steak Salad 51
  - Plum & Ginger Brisket 200
  - Southwestern Meatballs 205
  - Thai Beef Salad 57
  - Truffled Mushroom Silver Tip Roast 207
- beets
  - Moroccan Mint Beet Salad · 49
- bell peppers
  - 4 Bean & Kale Super Stew · 27
  - Ginger Brown Rice · 67
  - Moroccan Salmon ... Herb Relish 138
  - Nasi Goreng 176
  - Pepper Steak Salad 51
  - Pineapple Salmon Skewers 143
  - Rainbow Quesadilla Pizza · 123
  - Rosemary Lamb Skewers 203
  - Spanish Quinoa with Sausages 88
  - Thai Beef Salad 57
  - Vegetable Jalfrezi · 130
- Bhinidi Masala · 63
- Bhurtha · 101
- Biryani, Quinoa Veggie · 120
- blueberries
  - Blueberry Crumble · 215
  - Blueberry Scones · 11
- Bocaditos de Papa · 65
- bread
  - Irish Soda Corn Bread · 17
- breakfast section 8-23
- brisket
  - Plum & Ginger Brisket 200
- Brussels sprouts
  - Irish Garlic Brussels Sprouts · 71
- butternut squash
  - Butternut Squash Gnocchi · 102
  - Vegetable Dhansak · 129
- cake
  - Banana Walnut Cake · 212
  - Irish Apple Cake · 227
  - Tiramisu · 213
- Cambodian
  - Coconut Chicken ... Plum Sauce 161
- candied
  - Candied Fig and Goat Cheese Salad · 33
  - Candied Pecans · 33
- cauliflower
  - Aloo Gobi · 99
  - Quinoa Veggie Biryani · 120
  - Vegetable Jalfrezi · 130
  - Veggie Pakoras · 95
- Chana Masala · 105
- Chestnut Soup · 34
- chicken
  - Baked Chicken with Apple & Fennel 153
  - Chicken Breasts ... Fig-Mustard Glaze 155
  - Chicken Tikka Masala 156
  - Chicken with Mango Ginger Chutney 158
  - Coconut Chicken ... Plum Sauce 161
  - Coq au Vin with Saffron Quinoa 163
  - Garlic & Almond Chicken 167

- Grilled Chicken ... Spicy Mango Salsa 169
- Lemongrass Chicken Skewers 171
- Mandarin Orange Chicken Salad 46
- Mediterranean Chicken 173
- Moroccan Chicken 174
- Nasi Goreng 176
- Pad Thai 179
- Pineapple Mint Chicken 180
- Tandoori Chicken 182
• chickpeas
- 4 Bean & Kale Super Stew · 27
- Chana Masala · 105
- Indian Spiced Roasted Chickpeas · 68
• Chinese
- Tofu in Black Bean Sauce · 126
• chips
- Plantain Chips · 82
• chocolate
- Bailey's Irish Mousse · 211
- Chocolate Mousse Pie · 217
• Churros · 218
• Classic Crème Brûlée · 221
• coconut
- Coconut Cream Parfait · 222
- Coconut Chicken ... Plum Sauce 161
- Coconut Da'al · 107
- Coconut Pancakes · 13
- Coconut Sticky Rice with Mango · 224
• Coq au Vin with Saffron Quinoa 163
• corn
- Black Bean & Corn Salad · 31
- Creamed Corn Topping · 135
- Irish Soda Corn Bread · 17
- Mexican Street Corn · 79
- Nutty Corn Pancakes · 80
• Crêpes ... Lemon Curd & ... Berries · 15
• curries
- Aloo Gobi · 99
- Beef Korma 187
- Bhinidi Masala · 63
- Bhurtha · 101
- Chana Masala · 105
- Chicken Tikka Masala 156
- Curried Quinoa Salad ... Mint Raita · 37
- Curried Yam Soup · 39
- Keema 194
- Lamb Curry 197
- Palak Paneer · 117
- Tandoori Chicken 182
• da'al
- Coconut Da'al · 107
• dessert section · 208-231
• Diakon Radish Fries, Spicy · 91
• dips, sauces, chutneys & salsas ·
- Basil Yogurt Sauce 148
- Black Bean Sauce 126
- Creamed Corn Topping 135
- Fig-Mustard Glaze 155
- Garlic Aioli 147
- Herb Relish 138
- Mango Ginger Chutney 158
- Olive Tapenade 141
- Pistachio Mint Pesto 199
- Plum Dipping Sauce 161
- Spicy Mango Salsa 169
- Spinach & Arugula Pesto 118
• Duck à l'Orange 164
• Ecuadorian
- 4 Bean & Kale Super Stew · 27
- Banana Walnut Cake · 212
- Beef Tacos · 189
- Black Bean & Corn Salad · 31
- Bocaditos de Papa · 65
- Churros · 218
- Feta Cheese & Quinoa Salad · 41
- Fish Tacos with Creamed Corn 134
- Grilled Chicken with Spicy Mango Salsa ... 169
- Pineapple Salmon Skewers 143
- Plantain Chips · 82
- Plantain Crusted Red Snapper 145
- Rainbow Quesadilla Pizza · 123
- Spinach & Quinoa Fritters · 93
• eggplant
- Bhurtha · 101
- Eggplant Parmigiana · 108
- Eggplant Risotto · 111
- Layered Ratatouille · 72
- Vegetable Dhansak · 129
• eggs
- Nasi Goreng 176
- Onion Lover's Spinach Scramble · 20
- Shakshuka · 23
• English
- Blueberry Crumble · 215
- Blueberry Scones · 11
• Fajitas al Sombrero 191
• feta cheese
- Feta Cheese & Quinoa Salad · 41
- Mexican Street Corn · 79
- Shakshuka · 23
• French
- Candied Fig & Goat Cheese Salad · 33
- Chestnut Soup · 34
- Chicken Breasts ... Fig-Mustard Glaze 155
- Chocolate Mousse Pie · 217
- Classic Crème Brûlée · 221
- Coq au Vin with Saffron Quinoa 163
- Crêpes ... Lemon Curd & ... Berries · 15
- Duck à l'Orange 164
- Filet Mignon ... Herb & Garlic Rub 192
- Layered Ratatouille · 72
- Lemon Meringue Tart · 228

index continued...

- Pistachio Mint Crusted Rack of Lamb 199
- Sage & Onion Spaghetti Squash Soufflé · ... 125
- Sweet Potato Leek Soup · 54
- Truffled Mushroom Silver Tip Roast 207

• figs
- Candied Fig & Goat Cheese Salad · 33
- Chicken Breasts ... Fig-Mustard Glaze 155
- Moroccan Chicken 174

• Filet Mignon ... Herb & Garlic Rub 192
• fish section 132-149
• Fish Tacos with Creamed Corn 134
• Fries, Spicy Diakon Radish · 91
• fritters
- Bocaditos de Papa · 65
- Spinach & Quinoa Fritters · 93

• garlic
- Baby Bok Choy with Garlic & Ginger · 61
- Filet Mignon ... Herb & Garlic Rub 192
- Garlic Aioli · 147
- Garlic & Almond Chicken 167
- Garlic & Basil Spaghetti Squash · 112
- Irish Garlic Brussels Sprouts · 71
- Sesame Garlic String Beans · 87

• ginger
- Baby Bok Choy with Garlic & Ginger · 61
- Chicken with Mango Ginger Chutney 158
- Ginger Brown Rice · 67
- Maple Ginger Roasted Sweet Potatoes · 76
- Plum & Ginger Brisket 200

• Gnocchi, Butternut Squash · 102
• goat cheese
- Candied Fig & Goat Cheese Salad · 33
- Pomegranate & Goat Cheese Salad · 53

• Grilled Chicken with Spicy Mango Salsa 169
• Halibut al Spinachi 137
• Herb Relish · 138
• Indian
- Aloo Gobi · 99
- Beef Korma 187
- Bhinidi Masala · 63
- Bhurtha · 101
- Chana Masala · 105
- Chicken Tikka Masala 156
- Chicken with Mango Ginger Chutney 158
- Coconut Da'al · 107
- Curried Quinoa Salad ... Mint Raita · 37
- Garlic & Almond Chicken 167
- Indian Spiced Roasted Chickpeas · 68
- Keema 194
- Lamb Curry 197
- Lemon Jerra Rice · 74
- Malai Kofta · 115
- Palak Paneer · 117
- Quinoa Veggie Biryani · 120
- Saffron Rice · 85
- Spicy Diakon Radish Fries · 91
- Tandoori Chicken 182
- Vegetable Dhansak · 129
- Vegetable Jalfrezi · 130
- Veggie Pakoras · 95

• Indian Spiced Roasted Chickpeas · 68
• Indonesian
- Lemongrass Chicken Skewers 171
- Nasi Goreng 176
- Nutty Corn Pancakes · 80
- Pineapple Mint Chicken 180

• Irish
- Bailey's Irish Mousse · 211
- Irish Apple Cake · 227
- Irish Blue Potato Beef Stew 43
- Irish Garlic Brussels Sprouts · 71
- Irish Soda Corn Bread · 17

• Israeli
- Shakshuka · 23

• Italian
- Butternut Squash Gnocchi · 102
- Eggplant Parmigiana · 108
- Eggplant Risotto · 111
- Garlic & Basil Spaghetti Squash · 112
- Halibut al Spinachi 137
- Italian Wedding Soup 45
- Mediterranean Chicken 173
- Olive Tapenade Roasted Salmon 141
- Pasta with Spinach & Arugula Pesto · 118
- Rosemary Lamb Skewers 203
- Rosemary Walnut Salmon ... Garlic Aioli .. 147
- Tiramisu · 231
- Tuna Steaks ... Basil Yogurt Sauce 148

• Italian Wedding Soup 45
• kale
- 4 Bean & Kale Super Stew · 27

• Keema 194
• lamb
- Keema 194
- Lamb Curry 197
- Pistachio Mint Crusted Rack of Lamb 199
- Rosemary Lamb Skewers 203

• Layered Ratatouille · 72
• leeks
- Sweet Potato Leek Soup · 54

• lemons
- Crêpes ... Lemon Curd & ... Berries · 15
- Lemon Jerra Rice · 74
- Lemon Meringue Tart · 228
- Lemon Ricotta Pancakes · 19

• Lemongrass Chicken Skewers 171

- lentils
  - 4 Bean & Kale Super Stew · 27
  - Coconut Da'al · 107
  - Vegetable Dhansak · 129
- London broil
  - Thai Beef Salad 57
- Malai Kofta · 115
- Mandarin Orange Chicken Salad 46
- mangos
  - Chicken with Mango Ginger Chutney 158
  - Coconut Sticky Rice with Mango · 224
  - Curried Quinoa Salad ... Mint Raita · 37
  - Grilled Chicken ... Spicy Mango Salsa 169
- Maple Ginger Roasted Sweet Potatoes · 76
- masala
  - Bhinidi Masala · 63
  - Chana Masala · 105
  - Chicken Tikka Masala 156
- meat section 184-207
- meatballs
  - Italian Wedding Soup 45
  - Southwestern Meatballs 205
- Mediterranean Chicken 173
- Mexican
  - Mexican Street Corn · 79
- mint
  - Curried Quinoa Salad ... Mint Raita · 37
  - Mandarin Orange Chicken Salad 46
  - Moroccan Mint Beet Salad · 49
  - Pineapple Mint Chicken 180
  - Pistachio Mint Crusted Rack of Lamb 199
- Moroccan
  - Moroccan Salmon ... Herb Relish 138
  - Moroccan Chicken 174
  - Moroccan Mint Beet Salad · 49
- mousse
  - Bailey's Irish Mousse · 211
  - Chocolate Mousse Pie · 217
- mushrooms
  - Chestnut Soup · 34
  - Coq au Vin with Saffron Quinoa 163
  - Spinach & Quinoa Fritters · 93
  - Truffled Mushroom Silver Tip Roast 207
- Nasi Goreng 176
- Nutty Corn Pancakes · 80
- okra
  - Bhinidi Masala · 63
- olives
  - Feta Cheese & Quinoa Salad · 41
  - Mediterranean Chicken 173
  - Moroccan Salmon ... Herb Relish 138
  - Moroccan Chicken 174
  - Olive Tapenade Roasted Salmon 141
- onions
  - Onion Lover's Spinach Scramble · 20
  - Sage & Onion Spaghetti Squash Soufflé · ... 125
- oranges
  - Duck à l'Orange 164
  - Mandarin Orange Chicken Salad 46
- Pad Thai 179
- Palak Paneer · 117
- paneer cheese
  - Malai Kofta · 115
  - Palak Paneer · 117
  - Vegetable Jalfrezi · 130
- pancakes
  - Coconut Pancakes · 13
  - Lemon Ricotta Pancakes · 19
  - Nutty Corn Pancakes · 80
- Parfait, Coconut Cream · 222
- Parmigiana, Eggplant · 108
- pastas & noodles
  - Beef Pho 28
  - Butternut Squash Gnocchi · 102
  - Pad Thai 179
  - Pasta with Spinach & Arugula Pesto · 118
- peanuts
  - Nutty Corn Pancakes · 80
  - Pad Thai 179
- Pepper Steak Salad 51
- pie
  - Chocolate Mousse Pie · 217
- pineapples
  - Pineapple Mint Chicken 180
  - Pineapple Salmon Skewers 143
- Pistachio Mint Crusted Rack of Lamb 199
- pizza
  - Rainbow Quesadilla Pizza · 123
- plantains
  - Plantain Chips · 82
  - Plantain Crusted Red Snapper 145
- plums
  - Plum & Ginger Brisket 200
  - Coconut Chicken ... Plum Sauce 161
- Pomegranate & Goat Cheese Salad · 53
- potatoes (see sweet potatoes)
  - Aloo Gobi · 99
  - Bocaditos de Papa · 65
  - Irish Blue Potato Beef Stew 43
  - Malai Kofta · 115
  - Quinoa Veggie Biryani · 120
  - Vegetable Dhansak · 129
- poultry section 150-183
- pudding
  - Coconut Cream Parfait · 222
- Quesadilla Pizza, Rainbow · 123
- quinoa
  - Coq au Vin with Saffron Quinoa 163
  - Curried Quinoa Salad ... Mint Raita · 37
  - Feta Cheese & Quinoa Salad · 41
  - Italian Wedding Soup 45
  - Quinoa Veggie Biryani · 120

index continued...

- Spanish Quinoa with Sausages 88
- Spinach & Quinoa Fritters · 93
• Rainbow Quesadilla Pizza · 123
• Radish Fries, Spicy Diakon · 91
• Ratatouille, Layered · 72
• red snapper
- Fish Tacos with Creamed Corn 134
- Plantain Crusted Red Snapper 145
• rice
- Coconut Sticky Rice with Mango · 224
- Eggplant Risotto · 111
- Ginger Brown Rice · 67
- Lemon Jerra Rice · 74
- Nasi Goreng 176
- Saffron Rice · 85
• Risotto, Eggplant · 111
• rosemary
- Rosemary Lamb Skewers 203
- Rosemary Walnut Salmon ... Garlic Aioli .. 147
• saffron
- Coq au Vin with Saffron Quinoa 163
- Garlic & Almond Chicken 167
- Saffron Rice · 85
• sage
- Butternut Squash Gnocchi · 102
- Sage & Onion Spaghetti Squash Soufflé · ... 125
• salads
- Black Bean & Corn Salad · 31
- Candied Fig & Goat Cheese Salad · 33
- Curried Quinoa Salad ... Mint Raita · 37
- Feta Cheese & Quinoa Salad · 41
- Mandarin Orange Chicken Salad 46
- Moroccan Mint Beet Salad · 49
- Pepper Steak Salad 51
- Pomegranate & Goat Cheese Salad · 53
- Thai Beef Salad 57
• salmon
- Moroccan Salmon ... Herb Relish 138
- Olive Tapenade Roasted Salmon 141
- Pineapple Salmon Skewers 143
- Rosemary Walnut Salmon ... Garlic Aioli .. 147
• sausages
- Spanish Quinoa with Sausages 88
• scones
- Blueberry Scones · 11
• Scottish
- Baked Chicken with Apple & Fennel 153
• Sesame Garlic String Beans · 87
• Shakshuka · 23
• sides section 58-95
• Silver Tip Roast, Truffled Mushroom 207
• skewers
- Chicken Tikka Masala 156
- Lemongrass Chicken Skewers 171
- Pineapple Salmon Skewers 143
- Rosemary Lamb Skewers 203
• soups & salads section 24-57
• soups & stews
- 4 Bean & Kale Super Stew · 27
- Beef Pho 28
- Chestnut Soup · 34
- Coconut Da'al · 107
- Curried Yam Soup · 39
- Irish Blue Potato Beef Stew 43
- Italian Wedding Soup 45
- Lamb Curry 197
- Sweet Potato Leek Soup · 54
- Vegetable Dhansak · 129
- Vegetable Jalfrezi · 130
• Southwesten Meatballs 205
• spaghetti squash
- Garlic & Basil Spaghetti Squash · 112
- Sage & Onion Spaghetti Squash Soufflé · ... 125
• Spanish
- Spanish Quinoa with Sausages 88
• Spicy Diakon Radish Fries · 91
• Spicy Mango Salsa · 169
• spinach
- 4 Bean & Kale Super Stew · 27
- Coconut Da'al · 107
- Curried Quinoa Salad ... Mint Raita · 37
- Halibut al Spinachi 137
- Italian Wedding Soup 45
- Onion Lover's Spinach Scramble · 20
- Palak Paneer · 117
- Pasta with Spinach & Arugula Pesto · 118
- Pepper Steak Salad 51
- Spinach & Quinoa Fritters · 93
• Steak Salad, Pepper 51
• Sticky Rice with Mango, Coconut · 224
• string beans
- Sesame Garlic String Beans · 87
- Vegetable Jalfrezi · 130
• sweet potatoes
- 4 Bean & Kale Super Stew · 27
- Maple Ginger Roasted Sweet Potatoes · 76
- Sweet Potato Leek Soup · 54
• tacos & tortillas
- Beef Tacos 189
- Fajitas al Sombrero 191
- Fish Tacos with Creamed Corn 134
• Tandoori Chicken 182
• tart
- Lemon Meringue Tart · 228
• Thai
- Coconut Pancakes · 13

- Mandarin Orange Chicken Salad 46
- Pad Thai 179
- Pepper Steak Salad 51
- Plum & Ginger Brisket 200
- Thai Beef Salad 57
• Thai Beef Salad 57
• Tikka Masala, Chicken 156
• Tiramisu · 231
• Tofu in Black Bean Sauce · 126
• tomatoes
- Bhinidi Masala · 63
- Chana Masala · 105
- Chicken Tikka Masala 156
- Coconut Da'al · 107
- Eggplant Parmigiana · 108
- Layered Ratatouille · 72
- Mediterranean Chicken 173
- Palak Paneer · 117
- Shakshuka · 23
- Vegetable Dhansak · 129
- Vegetable Jalfrezi · 130
• Truffled Mushroom Silver Tip Roast 207
• tuna steaks
- Tuna Steaks ... Basil Yogurt Sauce 148
• Tuna Steaks ... Basil Yogurt Sauce 148
• Vegetable Dhansak · 129
• Vegetable Jalfrezi · 130
• vegetarian section 96-131
• Veggie Pakoras · 95
• Vietnamese
- Baby Bok Choy with Garlic & Ginger · 61
- Beef Pho 28
- Coconut Sticky Rice with Mango · 224
- Curried Yam Soup · 39
- Ginger Brown Rice · 67
- Sesame Garlic String Beans · 87
• walnuts
- Banana Walnut Cake · 212
- Blueberry Crumble · 215
- Pomegranate & Goat Cheese Salad · 53
- Rosemary Walnut Salmon ... Garlic Aioli .. 147
• yams
- Curried Yam Soup · 39
• zucchinis
- Ginger Brown Rice · 67
- Layered Ratatouille · 72